# Still Moving

The Film and Media Collections of The Museum of Modern Art

*Steven Higgins*

The Museum of Modern Art, New York

Produced by the Department of Publications
The Museum of Modern Art, New York

Edited by Emily Hall; Cassandra Heliczer
Designed by Antony Drobinski, Emsworth Design, Inc.
Cover designed by Gina Rossi
Production by Christina Grillo
Printed and bound by Editoriale Bortolazzi-Stei s.r.l, Verona

This book is typeset in Janson and Franklin Gothic.
The paper is 135gsm Gardapat Kiara.

Published by The Museum of Modern Art
11 West 53 Street, New York, New York 10019-5497
www.moma.org

Library of Congress Control Number: 2006928763
ISBN: 978-0-87070-326-3

Distributed in the United States and Canada by
D.A.P./Distributed Art Publishers, Inc., New York
Distributed outside the United States and Canada
by Thames & Hudson Ltd., London

Front cover:
Terence Davies
*The Long Day Closes*. 1992

Frontispiece:
Charles Chaplin
*The Tramp*. 1915

Back cover:
Ernie Gehr
*Serene Velocity*. 1970

Printed in Italy

# Contents

# Foreword

In 1935 The Museum of Modern Art established the Film Library, the first department in an American art museum dedicated to the collection, preservation, and exhibition of film as an art form. For at least a decade before that, the Museum's founding Director, Alfred H. Barr, Jr., had been deeply engaged in film culture, attending screenings whenever possible and meeting and corresponding with filmmakers in the United States and across Europe. As a result of this activity, Barr recognized early on that motion pictures were central to the modern experience, and he was determined to include them in any museum of art with which he might be associated. With the hiring of Iris Barry—a British film critic whose work Barr knew and respected and whose passion for and untiring efforts on behalf of the art of the cinema would become legendary—as the Museum's first curator of film and the appointment of Trustee and film-industry executive John Hay Whitney as the new Film Library's energetic first chairman, a solid foundation was laid for this new way of thinking about and presenting film.

Seventy years later, the Museum continues to honor Barr's original mission. Works on video emerged in the early 1970s and soon thereafter were welcomed into the permanent collections, as was media art over the last decade. In all, the Museum's permanent film and media collections now include more than twenty thousand individual works that span the history of the moving image—from W. K. L. Dickson and William Heise's *Blacksmithing Scene*, a twenty-seven-second Kinetoscope film made for Thomas Edison in 1893 and the first movie exhibited publicly in America, to *Owls at Noon Prelude: The Hollow Men*, an original media work by Chris Marker, which had its premiere in the Museum's new Yoshiko and Akio Morita Gallery in 2005.

*Still Moving: The Film and Media Collections of The Museum of Modern Art* is the first book about these collections to be published by The Museum of Modern Art. Over the years, many of the Museum's film and media exhibitions have been accompanied by publications of lasting merit, but never before has the scope of the permanent collections been presented in a single volume. Steven Higgins, author of this book and curator of the collections, has carefully chosen approximately five hundred images, most from the Museum's own extensive Film Stills Archive, in an effort to represent the remarkable riches of these holdings. In addition, his introduction and occasional short texts give the reader a sense of how the Museum goes about collecting, protecting, and exhibiting film and media.

Of course, a collection of this size and importance could not have been built without the efforts of many people, over many years. Chief among these are the many curators, past and present, who have dedicated their professional lives to acquiring and contextualizing for an interested public not only the acknowledged masterpieces of film and media history but also the important smaller works that would otherwise have been lost in the constant flood of moving images that overwhelm us on a daily basis. No less important are the Trustees, whose vision and generous support have enabled the Museum to remain one of the very few art museums anywhere in the world to collect and exhibit motion pictures on a par with painting, sculpture, and the other visual arts. It is a fact worthy of note that, well into film's second century, The Museum of Modern Art is still unusual in this respect, but it is also a fact of which we are justifiably proud, as well as being a tribute to the vision of our founders.

Glenn D. Lowry
*Director*
*The Museum of Modern Art*

# Preface

The Museum of Modern Art's film and media collections are some of the most important of their kind in the world. They span the history of the art of the moving image through every decade since its modern birth, from the last decade of the nineteenth century to the first decade of the twenty-first, from the films produced by the Edison and Biograph companies to the contemporary media of electronics and computers. The collections emphasize the American cinema, but are international, with works from six continents. They offer a vital support for scholars, students, and practitioners of this crucial aesthetic form of the modern period.

The founding curator of the collections—the first in any museum—was Iris Barry, who joined the Museum staff in 1935. The curatorial staff has continued to broaden the film and media collections up to the present day, enlarging them over the years to cover the medium's entire history, from directors who worked within the Hollywood studio system to individual artists who created deeply personal works, from Clint Eastwood to Stan Brakhage, from Martin Scorsese and Jean-Luc Godard to Shirley Clarke and Jim Jarmusch. Many filmmakers have donated works to the collections over the years, and the practice continues today—a measure of the recognition and importance accorded to the collections by the filmmaking community. Some of the most meaningful, indeed most wonderful, parts of my working life at the Museum have been my collaborations with other curators and with film and video artists in building the Museum's collections. There are so many works here that mean so much to me—by Hitchcock and Lubitsch and John Ford, by Warhol and Fassbinder, by video-makers such as Bill Viola and Yvonne Rainer and Joan Jonas.

The images in this book come almost entirely from a vital complement to the collection, the Film Stills Archive. *Still Moving* presents just a fragment of the Film Stills Archive, which in turn represents just a fragment of the larger collections. Even this fragment is rich enough, though, that no film scholar—no lover of the art of moving images—should be without this book.

Mary Lea Bandy
*Chief Curator Emerita*
*Department of Film and Media*

# Introduction

*My task which I am trying to achieve is…before all, to make you see.*

When Joseph Conrad wrote these words in 1897, motion pictures were barely four years old, and film culture—the projection of those motion pictures onto a screen before an audience—less than two.

During those earliest years, filmmakers aspired to do little more than document the physical world around them and reproduce popular entertainments from live theater. Their goal was to create an audience where none had existed before, to entertain the masses in such a way as to make the novelty of motion pictures an integral part of the world's precious leisure hours.

Within two decades of their initial efforts, the new film moguls had succeeded beyond such modest aims. Audiences throughout North America and Europe filled movie theaters every day, amusing themselves with a steady diet of melodramas, comedies, newsreels, and animation, and the rest of the world would soon follow. Virtually overnight, film studios appeared in cities around the world to meet audience demand, and what was at first a curious offshoot of vaudeville soon became a thriving industry in its own right. With success came notoriety and the attention of political and social elites, who began to weigh in on both the benefits and dangers of motion pictures as well as on their place in the wider cultural landscape. Soon a small but increasingly vocal number of filmmakers and critics were beginning to speak of film not simply as a means for entertaining the masses but as a new art form in its own right.

Although Conrad was writing about literature, his description of an artist as one who creates so that others might experience and understand what previously has been hidden or unknown was one that appealed to the ambitions of early filmmakers. Whether they did so out of aesthetic conviction or as a way to expand and deepen their economic and cultural stake in their communities, early film producers, directors, writers, and actors in Europe and America identified themselves increasingly not as mere showmen and entertainers but as artists.

Authors such as Vachel Lindsay and Hugo Munsterberg published books that supported this view, both making serious claims for film as a new and distinctively modern art, one that reflected the industrial and entrepreneurial society from which it arose. A popular art, one of the "seven lively arts," as Gilbert Seldes would write in 1924, but an art nonetheless.

By then, some individuals were taking up the banner of film as an art form with possibilities beyond narrative. Visual artists in Europe turned to theories of assemblage and montage to create abstract and nonnarrative films, works that would challenge audiences and critics alike to look at the motion picture as a natural outgrowth of painting and photography. Still other artists would take these same ideas and reapply them to narrative, thus closing the circle by demonstrating that montage and assemblage were tools that could be used in the service of traditional storytelling.

Conrad's self-described mission is one that might be readily expressed by any artist—or, for that matter, any curator. For those of us who work in museums, the goal is to acquire, care for, and present art so that others will not simply look at it (although there is value in that) but see it in a deeper, wider way.

## Acquisition

In 1932 Alfred H. Barr, Jr., the Museum's founding director, stressed the importance of introducing film, "the only great art form peculiar to the twentieth century," to "the American public which should appreciate good films and support them." Barr understood, before most others, that motion pictures belonged in a museum of *modern* art, that the simple fact of their emergence from the cultural ferment of the modern age gave them a place in such an institution. In 1935 he hired English film critic Iris Barry to be the first curator of the Museum's new Film Library, and John E. Abbott as its first director. Museum Trustee John Hay "Jock" Whitney—who, in addition to collecting modern painting, produced films in partnership with David O. Selznick—was chosen as the first chairman of the Film Library, a position he held from 1935 to 1951.

Then, as now, most films were controlled by large corporate interests, and so Whitney and Barr understood that the Museum's collection could only be assembled in cooperation with those who made the movies. Whitney sent Barry and Abbott to Hollywood to persuade industry leaders to donate prints, a radical concept that startled stars and producers alike. At a reception and screening at the Pickfair mansion in August 1935, attended by such industry power brokers as Harry Cohn, Merian C. Cooper, Samuel Goldwyn, Harry Warner, Jesse Lasky, Walter Wanger, and Walt Disney, Barry illustrated film's brief but important history with a short program of film clips, demonstrated the fragility of the medium, and argued the need to safeguard it. Soon afterward, donations of prints arrived in New York from Warner Bros., Paramount, Twentieth Century–Fox, Samuel Goldwyn, Harold Lloyd, Walt Disney, William S. Hart, Mary Pickford, Douglas Fairbanks, and David O. Selznick, among others.

In 1936 Barry traveled to Europe and the Soviet Union to acquire international films and meet filmmakers such as Sergei Eisenstein. So successful was this initial collection that in 1937 the Academy of Motion Pictures Arts and Sciences commended the Museum with an award "for its significant work in collecting films…and for the first time making available to the public the means of studying the historical and aesthetic development of the motion picture as one of the major arts."

Together with the pioneering film archives located in London, Paris, and Berlin, the Museum established the International Federation of Film Archives (FIAF) in 1938 and hosted the organization's first congress in New York the following year. Now headquartered in Brussels, FIAF has grown to a membership of more than 135 noncommercial institutions worldwide. Members are required to uphold a code of ethics that articulates the field's highest professional standards, thus facilitating communication and cooperation among its far-flung members.

In 1939, the same year that Whitney and Selznick released *Gone with the Wind*, The Museum of Modern Art opened its permanent home on West Fifty-third Street in Manhattan and launched the first museum-based film-exhibition program in America. With prompting from Lillian Gish, D. W. Griffith was persuaded to deposit his films and papers at the Museum, enabling the first major retrospective of a film artist to be assembled. *D. W. Griffith:*

*American Film Master* set the standard for the presentation and analysis of the masters of this new art form.

Today the permanent collection contains more than twenty thousand titles and ranks as the world's finest museum archives of international film, video, and media art. Works by the inventors of film narrative—the creators of its forms, genres, and technology—are the cornerstones of the collection, and every major artist of the silent era is represented, as are the innovators and masters of the sound era. Important works by animators, early avant-garde artists, and contemporary experimental filmmakers are also collected.

Video appeared in the permanent collections in the 1970s, almost as soon as artists began to use this less-expensive and more-flexible alternative to film. Virtually overnight this new medium established its own aesthetic, a "cool" feeling quite different from that of film, which tends to be described as "warm." In recent years, digital technology has supplanted analog in the creation of video, and single-channel video art, meant to be viewed primarily in theaters or dedicated "black box" galleries, while still a vibrant form, has ceded its prominence to sculptural media installations that incorporate the moving image in new and unexpected ways. These distinctions are not absolute, of course, as artists have worked and will continue to work in the mediums that suit their visions. No matter what form they may take in the future, artworks that utilize motion pictures will continue to be acquired, cared for, and exhibited by The Museum of Modern Art.

## Conservation

Motion picture film and videotape decay. The rate at which they do so varies depending on a great many factors, including the materials used in their manufacture, the way they are handled during projection and playback, and the conditions under which they are stored. Given proper handling, decomposition can be slowed, but it cannot be prevented. As soon as a film print or videotape leaves the laboratory, it begins its inevitable decline. This is the reality that haunts—and challenges—moving-image archivists and conservators the world over. We at the Museum have always gone about our work of collecting and exhibiting film, video, and media works with the knowledge that ours is an inherently unstable art form.

A film or video is truly a work of art only when it is exhibited; otherwise, it is simply a roll of acetate (or nitrate, or polyester) sitting on a shelf in a cold vault. At the same time, to exhibit a film without properly protecting it by creating new negatives and duplicate prints (or, in the case of video, by transferring it to a more stable tape format or digital file) is to ensure the eventual disappearance of these works through neglect.

For many years, archivists and scholars have attempted to quantify how much of the world's film heritage has been lost. Conservative estimates have claimed that fifty percent of the world's pre-1950 film production has been lost forever, including fully eighty percent of the films from the silent era. After 1950 the numbers improve, but the problems multiply with the proliferation of color and sound technologies. One need only open the lid on a can of film suffering from "vinegar syndrome" to know that the hope of stability promised by early safety-film stocks was premature at best, and the many dozens of early video formats that lie on shelves and in vaults all over the world, unavailable for viewing because the tapes and the machinery to play them are no longer being manufactured, attest to the ephemeral nature of the form. All moving-image formats require vigilance if they are to survive.

Modern film and media conservation is a testament to that vigilance, whether it is done by an underfunded, understaffed, nonprofit archive or in a Hollywood studio with all of its considerable financial resources. Having once seen each other as adversaries, commercial and nonprofit archives today have come to understand that they are partners in a never-ending effort. Indeed, were it not for cooperative initiatives such as that between the major American film archives (the Museum's among them) and Sony, where the latter's Columbia studio holdings have been systematically evaluated and preserved, films like *On the Waterfront*, *It Should Happen to You*, and *Fail-Safe* might not be available for future generations to study and enjoy. The final product of such conservation may be a pristine print, restored using the best surviving preprint materials (negatives and/or fine-grain masters) and resulting in a film that can look and sound better than it did when first released, or it may be a new print that cannot help but show the ravages of time—scratches, dirt, missing footage, poor sound. This is unavoidable, since often the only reason a film survives at all is because someone somewhere had the foresight or the luck to hold onto what proved to be the last remaining copy. Usually in the public domain, these "orphan films" are taken in and cared for by the nonprofit archives of the world. No apologies need be made for the condition of these films; we are lucky they survive at all.

This leads to a question of semantics. "Conservation" is an umbrella term that encompasses both restoration and preservation. The two latter terms are not synonymous; in fact, they can be two very different things. When a film is preserved, at the very minimum a new preservation negative is made, from which subsequent prints may be struck. Special care is taken in the making of the negative, and every effort is made to minimize the effects of wear and tear on the source material, often an old exhibition print. Special printing methods may be used in an attempt to eliminate scratches, and, given enough time and money, digital technology may be employed to correct flaws in either the image or the sound or both, but the final product is essentially a copy of the original source material, with its deepest flaws often still evident.

Restoration requires significantly more work. The objective is to bring the film back as closely as possible to its condition upon initial release, which can only be accomplished if an original or preservation negative already survives or if multiple prints of the subject exist. With such materials, the conservator is able to compare and combine elements into a reasonable approximation of the film's original release. In the case of silent films, intertitles may be damaged or missing, in which case original production records, copyright registration documents, or censorship reports may allow for the recreation of essential narrative information. Whatever the process, the conservator must work with a light touch, lest the final product reflect his or her preconceptions and tastes rather than the vision of the original filmmakers.

The restoration of a film always involves its preservation, but preserving a film does not always result in a restoration. Most important of all, a film has not been preserved unless the final product is a *film*—a series of sequentially exposed photographic images fixed in an emulsion on an acetate or polyester base. Transferring a movie to DVD or some other digital format, "digitally restored" or not, is neither restoration nor preservation. It may be a convenient and welcome addition to a home library, but it does nothing to ensure the continued existence of the film as a film.

In the case of video, the process is both simpler and more complicated—simpler because the best solution is usually a transfer to a high-end, currently viable format that can be used both for stable storage and future duplication; more complicated because the aesthetic choices involved can be difficult, sometimes impossible, to achieve. The differences between a moving image generated on video in 1970 and one recorded digitally to a file in 2006 are many and significant, and the tendency among technicians is to "correct" for those differences so that the old image looks somehow "better," or more pleasing to the eye. However, as in film, that is an artist's choice and not one available to a curator or a conservator. The goal is to save the original—if not in its physical condition, then at least in appearance, so that contemporary audiences may appreciate the impact of the original work.

The final element in conservation involves proper storage. In 1996 the Museum opened the Celeste Bartos Center for Film Preservation in Pennsylvania's Pocono Mountains, one hundred miles west of New York City. Its two buildings hold the sum total of the Museum's seventy years of film and video collecting, as well as the special collections that have been assembled to assist researchers in their explorations of film art and culture. A fuller description of the Center is included at the end of this volume's plate section.

## Exhibition

Whether drawn from its own collections or built around those of other institutions, the Museum's film- and media-exhibition programs are designed to present audiences with the finest examples of the moving image. As our permanent collections are international in scope, representing all genres and time periods, so too are our exhibitions.

In its earliest years, the Film Library was America's only exhibitor of film's then-brief history. Barry, in a 1937 report to the Museum's Board of Trustees, stated simply and clearly that the Museum's public film programs would seek "to achieve a consciousness of history and tradition within the new art of the motion picture," and she and her colleagues set about to do just that. In the first three years of its existence, the Film Library was in contact with over fifteen hundred organizations nationwide, more than one hundred of which rented the programs that Barry and her colleagues had organized under such broad themes as "A Short Survey of the Film in America, 1895–1932" and "The Film in France." This circulating program was in keeping with similar initiatives in other of the Museum's curatorial departments, all of which were designed to promote modern art through touring exhibitions as well as within its own walls. With the opening of the West Fifty-third Street building in 1939, the Film Library acquired a dedicated theater, now known as the Roy and Niuta Titus Theater 1, in which to present its rapidly growing archive on a regular basis.

A second theater (Titus 2) was opened in the mid-1980s, with a third (the Celeste Bartos Theater) slated to appear in late 2006, and the film-exhibition program has grown to include video and digital media, both of which are presented in the new Yoshiko and Akio Morita Gallery, on the second floor of the new Museum building designed by architect Yoshio Taniguchi and opened in November 2004. Together these venues house the most-diverse and longest-running film- and media-exhibition programs in America.

As with other curatorial departments, the Museum's film and media exhibitions are often made up of works on loan from other institutions or individuals. The Museum regularly screens films from FIAF-member archives, as well as from studio and personal collections, and in so doing it readily acknowledges the fact that, unlike seventy years ago, when film was but four decades old, the Museum's archive cannot possibly hope to contain the entire depth and breadth of moving-image history.

In addition to numerous onetime exhibitions devoted to individual filmmakers or national cinemas, the Museum presents a wide variety of annual series such as *New Directors/New Films*, organized in cooperation with the Film Society of Lincoln Center and dedicated to presenting the finest new work by directors not already familiar to New York audiences; *To Save and Project: The MoMA International Festival of Film Preservation*, which, as its title suggests, offers the latest preserved films from archives around the world; and *Documentary Fortnight*, a showcase for compelling work in that genre. Offering up to six concurrent film and media series each month, averaging four screenings a day, six days a week, the Museum continues to take seriously Barry's early determination to foster in its audiences an appreciation of international film culture.

## Education

Broadly defined, the work of any curatorial department in any museum is educational in nature. Since the inception of the Film Library, the Museum has been dedicated to expanding its reach beyond its theaters through its circulating-film and archival-loan programs, as well as through participation in the activities of the Department of Education. Regular educational programs include, among others, *Friday Night at the Movies*, a semester-long thematic film series offered to New York City high school students in which lively discussions about the narrative content of films often lead to a deeper appreciation of cinematic form and grammar, and *Watch This!* and *Family Films*, both designed to create conversations between young children and their parents based on the viewing of short films and videos, with short accompanying talks by professionals in the field.

The Museum maintains a separate study center for film and media, distinct from its library and archives. Voluminous newspaper- and periodical-clipping files, a strong collection of key reference works, facilities for personal film and video viewing, and, not least, a curatorial staff dedicated to the dissemination of knowledge about the moving image in all its forms have made the Museum one of the world's leading centers for film and media study. Our special collections include original manuscripts, scripts, posters, rare books and periodicals, graphic materials, and a wide array of film ephemera, as well as one of the largest collections of film stills in the world, all of which are available to the serious student or researcher. The history of the moving image would be incomplete without such rich contextual materials.

This book is not a history of film, nor is it a complete visual record of the Museum's film and media collections. As already noted, those collections currently hold over twenty thousand works, and so for every film and video included in the plate section and checklist of this book, forty-five others have had to be left out—not because they are unworthy of note but because difficult choices had to be made. In the end, I have tried to represent the riches of the film and media collections through a careful selection of compelling images that will give the reader a better sense of just how wondrous these holdings are. A number of short texts are placed throughout, offering background information about key films and significant collections. My goal has been to give the reader a greater appreciation of what we do at The Museum of Modern Art and a clearer understanding of how we try our best "to make you see."

Steven Higgins
*Curator*
*Department of Film and Media*

# Acknowledgments

This book was begun at the urging of Mary Lea Bandy, longtime Chief Curator in the Department of Film and Media and my mentor and guardian angel in the world of film archiving. Throughout its planning and writing, I was supported by curatorial colleagues and friends across the entire Museum, many of whom offered encouragement and advice, all of it welcome and seriously considered. In particular, I must acknowledge Research Assistant Jenny He and Interns Brynn White and Maholo Uchida, all of whom worked as researchers and helped prepare the manuscript for editing. I also thank Associate Curator Barbara London and Assistant Curator Sally Berger for their help in securing and selecting the video images. In the Department of Publications, I was assisted by a talented and patient staff, chief among them Managing Editor David Frankel, Associate Editors Cassandra Heliczer and Emily Hall, and Associate Production Manager Christina Grillo. Tony Drobinski is responsible for the book's elegant design. This volume was produced under the guidance of Publishers Michael Maegraith and Christopher Hudson, and I thank them both for their encouragement and support. Finally, I thank my wife, Mary, and my son, Walker. They both listened as I deliberated with myself during the difficult task of image selection, shared my anxieties through the writing process, and generally reassured me as I worked numerous late nights and weekends. I could not wish for a better family.

Some of these texts are adapted from earlier writing, and I'd like to acknowledge those authors: Mary Lea Bandy for *His Girl Friday*, *Puissance de la parole*, *Unforgiven*, and *Screen Test: Jane Holzer*; Barbara London for *Three Transitions*, *Chott el-Djerid (A Portrait in Light and Heat)*, *Inasmuch As It Is Already Always Taking Place*, and *My New Theater 1*; and Laurence Kardish for *Text of Light*.

S. H.

# The Edison Collection

On October 8, 1888, Thomas A. Edison filed a caveat, a preliminary patent application, with the United States Patent Office, in which he claimed that he was "experimenting upon an instrument which does for the Eye what the phonograph does for the Ear, which is the recording and reproduction of things in motion, and in such form as to be both Cheap practical and convenient." Eight months later, he turned the project over to a team of technicians led by W. K. L. Dickson, a young Edison protégé working at the inventor's West Orange, New Jersey, plant. Of course, by the late nineteenth century, the principle of "persistence of vision" was well-known, having been the basis for numerous children's toys and optical novelties. Drawing on the groundbreaking photographic experiments of Eadweard Muybridge and Étienne-Jules Marey, as well as on George Eastman's success in developing a flexible celluloid film, Dickson and his colleagues devised the Kinetograph, the first successful motion picture camera, and the Kinetoscope, a

peephole viewing device, which they demonstrated to the public for the first time in 1893. Thus, movies were born.

The Edison Company released hundreds of short and feature-length films between 1893 and 1918, its final year of active film production. In its earliest years, Edison's films were brief recordings of real events, known as actualities, or of short fictional scenes. By 1902 longer narratives had begun to appear, such as *The Life of an American Fireman*, directed by Edwin S. Porter; the following year, Porter produced *The Great Train Robbery*, a drama- and spectacle-filled one-reel film that became the industry's first true blockbuster. Porter remained America's most successful and innovative filmmaker until the appearance of D. W. Griffith in 1908. From that time until its demise, the Edison Company continued to release well-made films that found consistent favor with audiences, even as the company gradually ceded the position of the nation's preeminent film studio to various rivals.

(continued on page 16)

W. K. L. Dickson and William Heise. **Blacksmithing Scene**. 1893

The Black Maria,
the world's first
film studio, c. 1893.

James White and
William Heise.
**Sun Dance—
Annabelle**. 1897.
*Annabelle Whitford*

Albert E. Smith.
**Burglar on the
Roof.** 1898.
Produced by the
American Vitagraph
Company and
distributed by Edison

*(continued from page 14)*

The Museum of Modern Art's Edison Collection consists of over 450 nitrate negatives and prints that were still in storage at the Edison factory in West Orange in 1940, when they were acquired with the help of R. L. Giffen. The films span the years 1896 through 1916, although the great majority of them fall between 1912 and 1915. The Museum's recent preservation of the films of this latter period reveals a body of work that can stand comparison with that of any studio of the time and demonstrates that, even seven decades after its acquisition, the Edison Collection contains treasures waiting to be unearthed and rediscovered.

*Left:*
James White and
William Heise.
**Fatima's Coochee-
Coochee Dance.**
1896. *Fatima*

*Above:*
Edwin S. Porter.
**The Life of an
American Fireman.**
1903. *James White*

Edwin S. Porter.
**The Great Train Robbery**. 1903.
*George Barnes*

*The Great Train Robbery* is not the earliest movie in which former showman and film exhibitor Edwin S. Porter told a story through the editing together of images in sequence, nor is it the first Western. Nevertheless, it is a milestone in American film history for its combination of the two elements into what was, at eleven minutes, an exceptionally long film for the time. In this silent movie, bandits hold up a train and rob passengers. After an escape and a chase on horseback, the bandits are caught. The outlaw fires his gun at the viewers as if they are passengers, in an extra shot that, Porter noted, could either be shown at the beginning or end of the film. With this single movie, Porter at once pulled the American film business out of its early doldrums and captured the imagination of the moviegoing public worldwide, using cameras mounted on moving trains, special optical effects, hand-colored images of gunshots and explosions, and trick photography—all the better to tell a story drawn blatantly from the popular dime novels and vaudeville of the day.

Edwin S. Porter.
**The Gay Shoe
Clerk.** 1903

Edwin S. Porter.
**Coney Island at
Night.** 1905

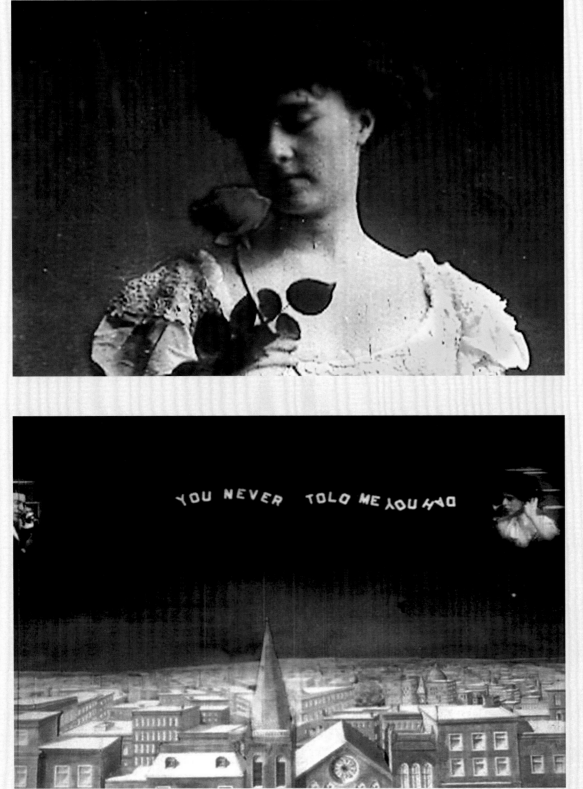

20

Edwin S. Porter.
**Three American
Beauties**. 1906

Edwin S. Porter.
**College Chums**.
1907. *Edward
Boulden, Miss Acton*

Left:
Edwin S. Porter
and Wallace
McCutcheon.
**The "Teddy"
Bears**. 1907

*Below:*
C. Jay Williams.
**The Totville Eye.**
1912

Ashley Miller.
**Children Who
Labor.** 1912

# Early Cinema

Louis Lumière.
**Sortie d'usine
(Workers Leaving
the Lumière
Factory)**. 1895

Louis and Auguste Lumière were already well-established photographers and manufacturers of photographic equipment when, in 1894, they witnessed a demonstration of Thomas Edison's Kinetoscope in Paris. Inspired by the American inventor's peepshow device, the Lumières quickly set out to create a combination camera, printer, and, most importantly, projector. Their new, simplified, and portable apparatus, which they called the "Cinématographe," had its world premiere in the Grand Café's Salon indien in Paris on December 28, 1895. The Lumière's first film (and one of several included in that initial program), *Sortie d'usine*, had been shot at their Lyon factory the previous June. As the *New York Dramatic Mirror* reported in its July 1896 review of the Cinématographe's U.S. premiere at Keith's Union Square Theatre, "the whistle blew, the factory doors were thrown open, and men, women, and children came trooping out. Several of the employees had bicycles, which they mounted outside the gate, and rode off.... A lecturer was employed to explain the pictures as they were shown, but he was hardly necessary, as the views speak for themselves, eloquently."

Louis Lumière.
**Repas de bébé
(Feeding the
Baby).** 1895.
*Auguste Lumière,
Mrs. Auguste
Lumière, and their
daughter*

Louis Lumière.
**L'Arroseur est
arrosé (Teasing
the Gardener).**
1895

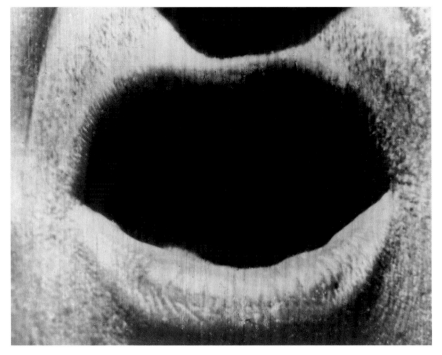

Louis Lumière.
**Arrivée d'un train
(à la Ciotat)
(Arrival of a Train
at La Ciotat).** 1895

James Williamson.
**The Big Swallow.**
1901

Georges Méliès.
**Le Voyage dans la lune (A Trip to the Moon)**. 1902

Charles Le Bargy and André Calmettes.
**L'Assassinat du Duc de Guise (The Assassination of the Duke de Guise)**. 1908

# The Biograph Collection

The founders of the American Mutoscope and Biograph Company (left to right: Henry Marvin, W. K. L. Dickson, Herman Casler, Elias B. Koopman), September 1895.

The American Mutoscope and Biograph Company was founded in 1896 by a consortium of businessmen that included W. K. L. Dickson, the man responsible for developing the first practical motion picture system for Thomas A. Edison earlier that decade. Biograph (as it came to be known) struggled for a number of years fighting off Edison's relentless litigation over alleged patent infringement until, in 1902, it became a licensee of the famous inventor's company. It was not until 1908, however, that Biograph finally became a significant challenge to Edison's dominance among American film producers.

In that year, an actor named D. W. Griffith joined Biograph, at first in front of the camera, and then behind it as a director and writer. Within six months of his directorial debut in the summer of 1908, Griffith established himself as a creative force in the American film industry and single-handedly stabilized Biograph's precarious financial situation by producing and releasing a regular schedule of popular films. Griffith worked at Biograph for five years (1908–13), during which time it became America's premiere film studio. When he left, after a disagreement with management over his desire to move from short- to feature-film production, Biograph quickly faded as a force in the industry. The studio ceased production in mid-1916, closing with an aborted series of films featuring the African American musical star Bert Williams.

The Biograph Company's motion picture negatives, business records, and salvageable equipment were put into storage until 1939, when Iris Barry, The Museum of Modern Art's first film curator, was asked by the Actinograph Corporation, a holding company, to take the material into the Museum's collections. Barry agreed, and the Biograph Collection—combined with the D. W. Griffith Collection acquired the previous year—became the heart of the Museum's new film archive. Preservation of the collection began almost immediately. The vast bulk of the

Biograph setup to film the Jeffries-Sharkey fight at the Coney Island Club House, New York, November 1899 (G. W. Bitzer, front left).

The first Biograph studio, on the roof of 841 Broadway, New York, c. 1897 (W. K. L. Dickson, second from right).

materials consisted of original camera negatives that were of a nonstandard "one hole" type unique to the Biograph Company, and that required the use of a specially adapted printing machine to transfer them to 35mm film stock. Former Biograph cameraman and Griffith collaborator G. W. "Billy" Bitzer assisted the Museum's staff in this project, resulting shortly thereafter in the first public exhibitions of Biograph films in nearly thirty years. In the decades since, and with the help of a generous bequest from Lillian Gish, the Museum has continued to preserve this precious cultural heritage for future generations.

The second Biograph studio, 11 East 14 Street, New York, c. 1909.

G. W. Bitzer (in wagon) during an 1899 trip to Boston, where local films were shot for exhibition at Keith's Union Square Theatre.

G. W. Bitzer.
**Interior N.Y.
Subway, 14th
Street to 42nd
Street.** 1905

When New York's Interborough Rapid
Transit system opened in October of
1904, it was hailed as an engineering mar-
vel, and people across America expressed
wonder and curiosity about what it was
like to move swiftly below the surface of
the nation's biggest and busiest city.
Within seven months of the subway's
opening, G. W. Bitzer provided an
answer, taking a Biograph camera underground to film this "actuality" film. The
bulky photographic apparatus was
mounted on the front of a train trailing
just behind the one being filmed, while a
flatcar filled with lights traveled on a par-
allel track, providing illumination in the
dark tunnel between Union Square and
the old Grand Central Station. The result
was an unprecedented view of the future
of urban travel in the new twentieth century. Although copyrighted and exhibited
on its own, footage from *Interior* was
included in another American Mutoscope
and Biograph Company release of 1905,
the comic farce *Reuben in the Subway*.

Wallace
McCutcheon.
**The Suburbanite.**
1904

G. W. Bitzer.
**Westinghouse
Works.** 1904

Wallace
McCutcheon.
**Falsely Accused!**
1908. *D. W. Griffith
(as a policeman, left,
hanging a screen)*

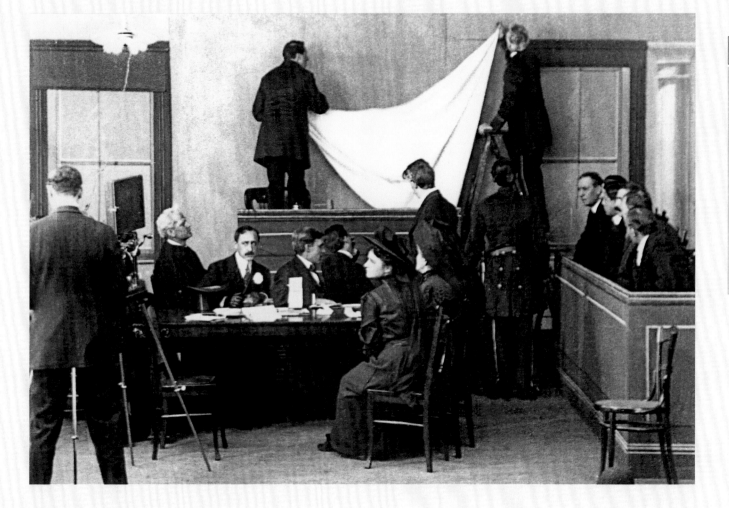

D. W. Griffith.
**The Country
Doctor**. 1909.
*Florence Lawrence,
Gladys Egan,
Frank Powell*

*The Country Doctor* is considered by many to be D. W. Griffith's first true masterwork. Filmed at the Biograph studio in New York and on location in Greenwich, Connecticut, in May and June of 1909, it tells the story of a well-to-do doctor who is torn between caring for a young girl who has fallen ill and his own daughter, who dies before he is able to return to her sickbed. As in his later "race to the rescue" films, in *The Country Doctor* Griffith cuts sharply between different physical locations to heighten dramatic tension; in this film, however, such cutting also creates an emotional bond between the audience and the doctor, allowing viewers to participate in his impossible choice between family and duty. The film opens and closes with a gentle pan across a rural landscape, a framing device that establishes an idyllic mood at the beginning but which is freighted with sadness at the end.

Filming D. W. Griffith's **The Cord of Life** in the Fourteenth Street Biograph studio, January 1909. *George Gebhardt (on stage, far left)*

D. W. Griffith. **Politician's Love Story.** 1909. *Mack Sennett, Marion Leonard*

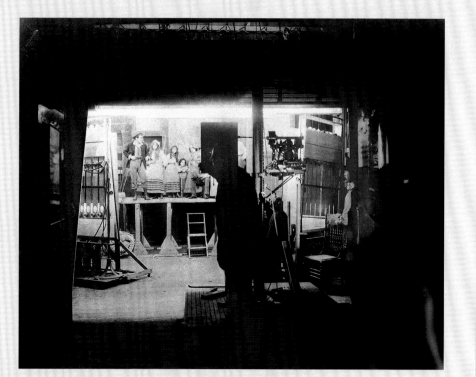

D. W. Griffith on
location in Westfield,
N. J., directing
**The Song of the
Wildwood Flute**,
with G. W. Bitzer
behind the camera,
October 1910.

34

Biograph factory
staff assembling
release prints,
c. 1909.

Biograph factory
staff checking
release prints,
c. 1909.

D. W. Griffith.
**The House with
Closed Shutters**.
1910. *Dorothy West,
Henry B. Walthall*

*Above*:
D. W. Griffith.
**The Mended
Lute**. 1909.
*James Kirkwood,
Florence Lawrence*

*Right*:
D. W. Griffith.
**The Lonely Villa**.
1909. *Adele De
Garde, Mary Pickford,
Gladys Egan, Marion
Leonard*

D. W. Griffith.
**A Corner in
Wheat**. 1909.
*Jeanie MacPherson
(far left), Frank
Powell (lying on
floor), Henry B.
Walthall (bent over),
Grace Henderson
(center), Frank
Evans (workman
standing right)*

A short film of near-perfect formal structure, *A Corner in Wheat* finds its sources in the paintings of the French artist Jean-François Millet (most notably *The Sower*, 1850), the writings of American author Frank Norris (especially his novel *The Octopus*, 1901, and short story "A Deal in Wheat," 1902), and the economic and social critiques of American capitalism made by progressives and socialists of the early twentieth century. Even without knowledge of such references, however, audiences have consistently been moved by D. W. Griffith's uncompromising indictment of reckless financial speculation, his clear affection for those who till the earth, and the sharp moral lessons he drew from the deft intercutting of these two very different yet intimately connected worlds.

Biograph's first
Los Angeles studio,
Grand Avenue and
Washington Street,
1910.

D. W. Griffith.
**What Shall We
Do with Our Old?**
1911. *Frank Evans,
Donald Crisp, Francis
J. Grandon (court
officers, left), George
O. Nicholls (judge),
W. Chrystie Miller
(elderly man)*

D. W. Griffith.
**The Battle.** 1911

*Left:*
D. W. Griffith.
**Fisher Folks.**
1911.
*Linda Arvidson*

*Below, left:*
D. W. Griffith.
**The Lonedale Operator.** 1911.
*Blanche Sweet*

*Below:*
D. W. Griffith.
**Her Awakening.**
1911.
*Mabel Normand, Harry Hyde*

D. W. Griffith.
**An Unseen
Enemy**. 1912.
*Dorothy Gish,
Lillian Gish*

As Lillian Gish remembered it, she and her sister Dorothy turned up at the Biograph studio one day in July of 1912 to visit their good friend Gladys Smith (better known in theater and film circles as Mary Pickford). In short order, the two young women met D. W. Griffith and were cast in this otherwise unremarkable melodrama about a pair of orphan girls who are menaced by thieves. A noteworthy example of Griffith's uncanny ability to make an entertaining film from slight material, *An Unseen Enemy* has become best known as the joint debut of two actresses who would soon become industry icons. A critic of the time acknowledged that although "not yet actresses," the Gish sisters gave "charming" performances in this one-reel film, adding that Biograph was "a good place to learn acting."

D. W. Griffith.
**The Mothering
Heart**. 1913.
*Lillian Gish*

D. W. Griffith.
**The New York
Hat**. 1912. *Lionel
Barrymore, Mary
Pickford, Charles
Hill Mailes*

On the set of
D. W. Griffith's
**Brute Force**,
c. May 1913.
*J. Jiquel Lanoe,
Dell Henderson,
Charles Hill Mailes,
Robert Harron
(seated), Mae Marsh,
William J. Butler,
Harry Hyde,
Alfred Paget,
D. W. Griffith,
W. Christy Cabanne
(in straw boater)*

D. W. Griffith.
**The Musketeers
of Pig Alley.** 1912.
*Lillian Gish,
Dorothy Gish,
Adolph Lestina*

D. W. Griffith set some of his most important Biograph films—*The Song of the Shirt* (1908), *Money Mad* (1908), *A Child of the Ghetto* (1910), *The Lily of the Tenements* (1911)—in the ghetto neighborhoods of New York City, and in this he was no different from many other filmmakers of the time. However, unlike most of his colleagues in the industry, who used such locations primarily as colorful backdrops for standard melodramas, Griffith sought to advance a markedly progressive agenda through these films, one that used melodrama to critique the systemic corruption and vice found in the inner city.

*The Musketeers of Pig Alley* (1912) was part of that cycle of films, but its story is also one of gang warfare and the honor of thieves, of life at its grittiest and most cynical—or, depending on one's point of view, most realistic. Oddly enough for a film heralded for years as being almost documentary-like in its depiction of the mean streets of the Lower East Side, careful comparison of the storefront scenes with other Biograph releases shows that the film was actually shot in Fort Lee, New Jersey—testimony to Griffith and cinematographer G. W. Bitzer's creative use of set dressing and camera placement.

44

D. W. Griffith.
**Judith of Bethulia.**
1914. *Blanche Sweet*

D. W. Griffith.
**The Battle at
Elderbush Gulch.**
1913

The Biograph
studio, 807 East
175 Street, Bronx,
N.Y., c. 1913.

Over the course of its twenty-year history, the American Mutoscope and Biograph Company occupied three studios in New York City: its first home was at 841 Broadway (on the corner of Thirteenth Street), where W. K. L. Dickson built a rooftop stage that moved on a system of tracks to catch the sunlight (as did The Black Maria, the studio he built in New Jersey for Thomas Edison); its second was a brownstone at 11 East 14 Street (home base for D. W. Griffith throughout his career with the company); the third was a building at 807 East 175 Street, in the Bronx, which opened in 1913 and was used by Biograph until the company shut down, three years later. Ironically, although the studio was built with profits amassed by the company during Griffith's successful tenure as head of production for Biograph, Griffith only used it to shoot a few minor scenes for *Judith of Bethulia* (1914), his last release for the company.

Georges Méliès.
**À la conquête du pôle (Conquest of the Pole).** 1912

Louis Mercanton.
**Les Amours de la reine Élisabeth (Queen Elizabeth).** 1912. *Lou Tellegen, Sarah Bernhardt*

Lois Weber and
Phillips Smalley.
**Suspense**. 1913.
*Sam Kaufman,*
*Valentine Paul,*
*Lois Weber*

The story of *Suspense* is a simple one—a tramp threatens a mother and child, while the father races home to their rescue—but the techniques used to tell it are complex. The writing/directing team of Lois Weber and Phillips Smalley employed a dizzying array of formal devices: the approach of an automobile is shown reflected in another car's side-view mirror; we catch our first glimpse of the menacing burglar from the same angle as the wife—from directly overhead as he glares straight up; three simultaneous actions are shown, not sequentially but as a triptych within a single frame. By the time they made this film, Weber and Smalley had sole responsibility for the output of Rex, an independent film company based in New York. *Suspense* is one of only three-dozen surviving Rex films, and its exceptional originality raises a beguiling question: is the film a fascinating anomaly, or is it a representative sample of the studio's overall production?

Mack Sennett.
**Barney Oldfield's
Race for a Life**. 1913.
*Mabel Normand, Ford
Sterling (with mallet)*

Winsor McCay.
**Gertie the
Dinosaur**. 1914

Cecil B. DeMille.
**The Squaw Man**.
1914. *Red Wing,
Dustin Farnum*

Mack Sennett.
**Tillie's Punctured
Romance**. 1914.
*Mabel Normand,
Charles Chaplin,
Marie Dressler,
Edgar Kennedy
(waiter)*

Charles Chaplin.
**The Tramp**. 1915.
*Charles Chaplin*

Gustavo Serena.
**Assunta Spina**.
1915. *Francesca Bertini*

*Above:*
Raoul Walsh.
**Regeneration**.
1915. *Anna Q. Nilsson, William Sheer*

*Left:*
Donald Mackenzie and Louis Gasnier.
**The Perils of Pauline**. 1914.
*Pearl White, Crane Wilbur*

Lloyd Ingraham.
**Hoodoo Ann**.
1916. *Mae Marsh,
Elmo Lincoln, and
Robert Harron
(sixth, seventh, and
eighth from left,
respectively)*

William S. Hart.
**Mr. "Silent"
Haskins**. 1915.
*Rhea Mitchell,
William S. Hart*

"THE COWARD" ©1915, TRIANGLE PLAYS.

Reginald Barker.
**The Coward**.
1915. *Charles Ray,*
*Frank Keenan*

This five-reel feature, produced by
Thomas H. Ince for the Triangle Motion
Picture Company and directed by Reginald
Barker, is a sophisticated psychological
portrait of cowardice set during the Civil
War. Popular stage star Frank Keenan, in
his first film role, portrays the cold and
forbidding father who assumes his son's
place in the ranks of the Confederate
army when the young man flees his first

battle. Charles Ray, who had been acting
in short films at the Inceville studios for
two years when this film came his way,
plays the son. Planned as a vehicle for
Keenan, *The Coward* became Ray's break-
through role instead, one that firmly
established his most popular on-screen
persona: that of the troubled yet well-
meaning youth who must prove his mettle
under trying circumstances.

Roscoe Arbuckle.
**Fatty and Mabel
Adrift**. 1916. *Roscoe
"Fatty" Arbuckle,
Mabel Normand*

Roscoe "Fatty" Arbuckle and Mabel
Normand were among the most popular
comedy teams in American cinema during
its early years. By the time *Fatty and
Mabel Adrift* was released, at the beginning of 1916, they had appeared together
as husband and wife or as eagerly flirta-
tious lovers in numerous productions for
Mack Sennett's Keystone Film Company,
most of them directed by Arbuckle himself. Although still an absurdly knock-
about comedy, this film is punctuated by
small, wistful moments that reveal
Arbuckle's growing ambitions as a director
outside of the Keystone mold. In fact,
Sennett and Arbuckle's creative relationship had become so strained that the
producer shipped Arbuckle and his company off to Keystone's facility at Fort Lee,
New Jersey, upon the film's completion.
There Arbuckle made six films before
returning west and leaving Sennett for his
own studio (Comique) and independence.

William S. Hart and
Charles Swickard.
**Hell's Hinges**.
1916. *William S.
Hart*

Thomas H. Ince and
Raymond B. West.
**Civilization**. 1916.
*Howard Hickman,
Charles K. French
(background), Herschel
Mayall, Lola May*

THOS. H. INCE'S
"CIVILIZATION"

SHIPMAN
FROM THE FILM
PROCESS

# The D. W. Griffith Collection

D. W. Griffith.
**Home Sweet
Home**. 1914.
*Karl Brown*

By the time he left the Biograph
Company in 1913, D. W. Griffith's
films were the most critically acclaimed and
popular of the era, but because Biograph
insisted that cast and crew not be identified
publicly, very few people knew the filmmaker's
name. By early 1915, however, with the release
of *The Birth of a Nation*, based on Thomas
Dixon's novel *The Clansman*, Griffith had
become the most visible film artist of his day.
His undeniable talent for both broad spectacle
and intimate melodrama, combined with a
showman's knack for self-promotion—all
gleaned from many years of trouping through
America as an actor and writer—served him
well as he proselytized energetically for film's
status as the world's newest and most powerful
art form. In 1919 he joined forces with Mary
Pickford, Douglas Fairbanks, and Charles
Chaplin to form United Artists, causing one
wag to remark, "The inmates have taken over
the asylum." What Griffith and his partners
understood, earlier than most, was that only by
taking hold of their creative and financial des-
tinies could they hope to make film more than
just another form of cheap amusement. In the
end, Griffith's financial acumen was not as keen
as his filmmaking talent, and he was forced to
give up his independence in the mid-1920s to
work for Paramount. A brief return to form in

the early sound period (with *Abraham Lincoln*,
1930) was followed by the failure of *The Struggle*
(1931), and Griffith's career came to an end. By
1938 D. W. Griffith Inc. was in receivership.

It was in that year that Lillian Gish, one of
Griffith's greatest stars, convinced him to transfer the films still in his possession to The
Museum of Modern Art. His lawyer, Woodson
R. Oglesby, negotiated an arrangement whereby
the Museum would pay all the storage fees
Griffith owed in exchange for permission to
exhibit the films and distribute them to nonprofit and educational institutions. With the
acquisition of the Biograph Collection the following year, Iris Barry was able to mount a
major exhibition covering Griffith's entire
career: in 1940 *D. W. Griffith: American Film
Master* opened at the Museum's new home on
West Fifty-third Street. An influential mono-
graph of the same name, authored by Barry,
accompanied the exhibition. After nearly a decade
of creative inactivity, during which the public's
perception of Griffith as a failed filmmaker had
hardened into reality, the Museum's acquisition
and exhibition of his groundbreaking body of
work convincingly demonstrated that, at his best,
Griffith was an artist of the first rank, worthy of
recognition by a museum of art.

D. W. Griffith.
**The Avenging Conscience**. 1914.
*Blanche Sweet*

This psychological thriller, D. W. Griffith's last film before he embarked on his production of *The Birth of a Nation* (1915), is justly famous for its evocation of Edgar Allan Poe's gothic milieu, as well as for Henry B. Walthall's powerful performance as a man driven to murder and insanity. Lifting elements from Poe's nineteenth-century story "The Tell-Tale Heart" and poem "Annabel Lee," *The Avenging Conscience* strives mightily for its horrific effects, largely achieving them while still falling victim to a certain stiffness, the result of an overly respectful reliance on its literary sources. Still, this eerie chamber piece is a strong example of Griffith's non-epic mode, and, in retrospect, may be seen as the perfect bridge between the jewel-like miniatures of his Biograph period (1908–13) and the sweeping ambitions of *The Birth of a Nation*, *Intolerance* (1916), and *Orphans of the Storm* (1921).

D. W. Griffith.
**The Birth of a Nation**. 1915.
*Henry B. Walthall*

D. W. Griffith.
**Intolerance**
("Babylonian
story"). 1916

D. W. Griffith.
**Intolerance** ("Out
of the cradle end-
lessly rocking. . .").
1916. *Lillian Gish*

D. W. Griffith.
**Intolerance**
("Modern story").
1916. *Mae Marsh*

D. W. Griffith.
**Intolerance**
("Christ story").
1916. *Howard Gaye
(as Christ)*

D. W. Griffith.
**Intolerance** ("St.
Bartholomew's Day
Massacre"). 1916

D. W. Griffith.
**Hearts of the
World**. 1918.
*Dorothy Gish,
Noel Coward*

When, in early 1917, the British government offered D. W. Griffith the opportunity to depict in motion pictures "an authentic history of the World War," he readily accepted and sailed for England, soon to be followed by G. W. Bitzer, Robert Harron, and the Gish sisters. Although Griffith remained in Europe until the autumn, shooting scenes with the cooperation of the War Office, the great majority of *Hearts of the World* was actually shot in Hollywood. It was initially conceived as a film to help convince America to enter the war on the side of the Allies, but production lagged (Griffith famously claimed that, as drama, the real war was boring); by the time of the movie's premiere in March of 1918, the U.S. had been at war for almost a year. In the end, *Hearts of the World* was a commercial success anyway, due in large part to its patriotic fervor, its director's unfailing ability to mesh quiet sentiment and thrilling action, and the spirited performance of Dorothy Gish as The Little Disturber.

D. W. Griffith.
**True Heart Susie**.
1919. *Lillian Gish*

D. W. Griffith.
**Broken Blossoms**.
1919. *Richard
Barthelmess,
Lillian Gish*

D. W. Griffith.
**Orphans of the Storm**. 1921.
*Monte Blue, Lillian Gish (on scaffold)*

After the box office failure of *Dream Street* (1921), a visually adventurous film that could not find an audience, Griffith turned to a theatrical warhorse for his next project, much as he had done for his last hit, *Way Down East* (1920). Griffith personally crafted the script by combining *Les Deux Orphelines*, a popular French melodrama that had its American premiere in 1874 as *The Two Orphans*, with the historical epic of the French Revolution. Fourteen acres of sets were built on the property surrounding the Mamaro-neck studio, and enormous research on the period was undertaken in order to provide the kind of authenticity that audiences had come to expect from Griffith. The result is Griffith's last undisputed masterwork (and the last time its costars, Lillian and Dorothy Gish, would ever work on a film together, or with their mentor, again). The film was a critical and popular success, but its enormous exploitation costs and unexpected road-show losses left Griffith and his company in even deeper debt than before.

D. W. Griffith.
**Way Down East**.
1920. *Richard
Barthelmess,
Lillian Gish*

D. W. Griffith.
**The White Rose**.
1923. *Mae Marsh*

D. W. Griffith. **Isn't Life Wonderful**. 1924. *Carol Dempster (third from left)*

D. W. Griffith. **Lady of the Pavements**. 1929. *Lupe Velez, William Boyd*

D. W. Griffith.
**Abraham Lincoln.**
*1930. Walter Huston*

Charles Chaplin.
**The Floorwalker**.
1916. *Charles Chaplin,*
*Eric Campbell*

Charles Chaplin.
**The Pawnshop**.
1916. *Charles Chaplin,*
*Albert Austin*

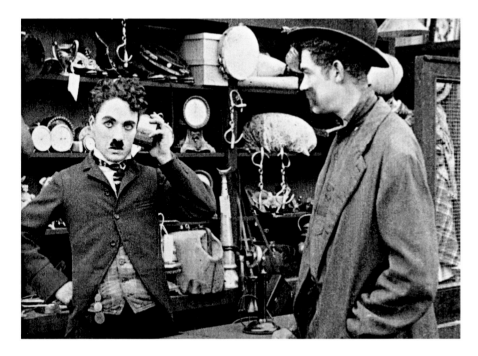

When Charles Chaplin signed with
Mutual in February of 1916 for the
unheard-of price of $670,000 for a single
year's work, audiences and journalists
around the world were aghast. Surely no
one could be worth $10,000 a week plus a
bonus of $150,000 simply for signing a
piece of paper. Chaplin proved the critics
and doubters wrong, producing a dozen
near-perfect two-reel comedies in seventeen months (the delay was due to illness
and his increasingly fastidious working
methods). *The Pawnshop*, the sixth film in
Chaplin's Mutual series, is made up of an
uninterrupted sequence of brilliant comedy routines, all set within the confines of
a simple pawnbroker's shop. The scene
illustrated here is the most famous. Chaplin evaluates a customer's alarm clock by
destroying it and then rejecting it as no
good. Albert Austin, an old colleague of
Chaplin's from his English music hall
days, played the customer.

Charles Chaplin.
**The Immigrant**.
1917. *Eric Campbell,*
*Charles Chaplin,*
*Edna Purviance,*
*Henry Bergman*

John Ford.
**Straight Shooting.**
1917

Victor L. Schertzinger.
**The Clodhopper**.
1917. *Margery Wilson,
Charles Ray*

Leopold Wharton.
**Patria**. 1917.
*Irene Castle*

William S. Hart.
**Branding Broadway**.
1918. *William S. Hart*

In this atypical 1918 comedy, William S. Hart is the leader of a band of cowboys intent on tearing up a "dry" Arizona town. Having caused more havoc than usual, he is tied up by the townspeople and put on a train bound for New York, where he becomes the guardian of a millionaire's son. Louis Reeves Harrison, reviewer for the *Moving Picture World*, wrote that it was "a pleasure to see Hart in an entirely new role" and declared the film "extravagant almost to the point of farce." Filled with plenty of stunts and physical action, including a large fight scene set in an elegant New York City restaurant and a chase on horseback up Sixth Avenue and into Central Park, *Branding Broadway* certainly offered enough action to satisfy any audience of Hart fans, but it also poked fun at his "two gun" persona, something that was as welcome as it was unexpected.

Clarence G. Badger.
**Jubilo**. 1919. *Josie
Sedgwick, Will Rogers*

Erich von Stroheim.
**Blind Husbands**.
1919. *Francelia
Billington, Erich
von Stroheim, T. H.
Gibson-Gowland,
Sam de Grasse*

*Opposite:*
Cecil B. DeMille.
**Male and Female**.
1919. *Gloria Swanson*

# 1920s

Paul Strand and
Charles Sheeler.
**Manhatta.** 1921

Henry King.
**Tol'able David**.
1921. *Richard
Barthelmess*

Director Henry King spent his early show business career trouping through the American heartland in vaudeville, circus, burlesque, and stock, eventually becoming an actor for the Lubin Company, in Philadelphia, in 1912. He soon switched to directing, working for a variety of producers before finding success with Thomas H. Ince, and in 1921 he cofounded Inspiration Pictures with the actor Richard Barthelmess. *Tol'able David*, about a sensitive young boy who endures the abuse of a brutal neighboring family as well as accusations of cowardice from his fellow townsfolk, was their first and greatest success. The screenplay, based on the story by the popular author Joseph Hergesheimer, was adapted by King and Edmund Goulding. King imbued the film with an affection for rural life that is untainted by false sentiment and which is based on his own observations of American types, made while traveling the country as an actor. Barthelmess drew upon his experience as a member of D. W. Griffith's stock company to breathe life into the character of David, an innocent dreamer who must grow up all too quickly.

Frank Borzage. **Humoresque**. 1920. *Vera Gordon, Bobby Connelly*

Leopold Jessner and Paul Leni. **Hintertreppe (Backstairs)**. 1921. *Henny Porten*

Nosferatu 33.                                    Prana-Film.

F. W. Murnau.
**Nosferatu: Eine Symphonie des Grauens**. 1922.
*Max Schreck*

Buster Keaton and
Edward Cline.
**Cops**. 1922.
*Buster Keaton*

Erich von Stroheim.
**Foolish Wives.**
1922

Fred Niblo.
**Blood and Sand**.
1922.
*Rudolph Valentino*

*Blood and Sand* stars Rudolph Valentino as the bullfighter Juan Gallardo, a man torn between the upright Carmen and the vampish Doña Sol. Chafing under the constraints of a screen career that, although barely a few years old, was already type-casting him as The Latin Lover, Valentino lobbied hard to make this film, which he hoped would make use of his physical poise and grace in support of a character and story of real substance. *Blood and Sand* proved to be less weighty than its star had hoped, but it was stylish fun and became a box office smash, catapulting Valentino to even greater popularity.

Robert J. Flaherty.
**Nanook of the
North**. 1922

When Robert Flaherty proposed filming an Inuit hunter and his family for a year, following them from igloo to igloo and from kill to kill in the harsh Arctic waste, no American movie company was willing to finance the project. In the end, the French furrier Revillon Frères backed the project, and the American branch of the French film company Pathé agreed to distribute it. The result was a film that may fairly be described as the foundation of the documentary genre. *Nanook of the North* went far beyond the actualities and travelogues of early cinema to present something new, a fictionalized version of a real person's life. Taking his cues from successful Hollywood films, Flaherty blended realistic and beautifully composed images with a loose narrative and a strong central character. While not, strictly speaking, an objective record of actual events, the work that emerged was nevertheless true to the spirit of the life it was trying to convey. Ever since *Nanook of the North* premiered, documentary filmmakers have been grappling with issues of objectivity versus subjectivity and reality versus invention that the film (unintentionally) raised.

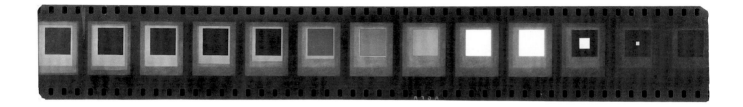

Hans Richter.
**Rhythmus 21.**
1921

Ernst Lubitsch.
**Rosita**. 1923.
*Mary Pickford*

*Above:*
King Vidor.
**Peg o' My Heart**.
1922. *Lionel Belmore,
Laurette Taylor,
Russell Simpson*

*Above, right:*
John Griffith Wray.
**Anna Christie**.
1923. *Blanche Sweet,
George F. Marion*

*Right:*
Arthur Robison.
**Schatten (Warning
Shadows)**. 1923

Buster Keaton and
John G. Blystone.
**Our Hospitality**.
1923. *Buster Keaton,
Natalie Talmadge*

Jean Epstein.
**Coeur fidèle**.
1923. *Gina Manès*

Abel Gance.
**La Roue**. 1923.
*Séverin-Mars*

Buster Keaton.
**Sherlock, Jr**. 1924.
*Buster Keaton*

Throughout his movie career, Buster
Keaton celebrated and drew on his long
years touring the country as a vaudeville
performer, while at the same time experimenting with the technical possibilities of
film like a child with a new toy. Nowhere
is this combination of elements more pro-
nounced than in *Sherlock, Jr.*, a simple tale
of a theater projectionist's efforts to prove
himself innocent of the theft of a watch,
and thereby win the hand of his sweet-
heart. In the middle of this plot, Keaton
and his writers present a dream sequence
in which the projectionist finds himself
transported into the film he has been projecting on-screen. He becomes the world-
famous detective Sherlock, Jr., a man who
can solve any case and who is capable of
amazing feats of physical daring. As in all
his films, Keaton is careful to demonstrate
that he, and not some stand-in, is doing
all of the stunts. That, as well as his habit
of staging his stunts frontally (to assure
the audience that no camera trickery is
involved), makes those moments when he
does play with the camera all the more
wondrous.

# The Douglas Fairbanks Collection

John Emerson.
**Wild & Woolly**.
1917. *Eileen Percy,
Douglas Fairbanks*

Despite his boyish amiability and athletic charm, Douglas Fairbanks was no youngster when he began his movie career in 1915. Born and raised in Colorado, Fairbanks left high school at seventeen to come east with his family, at which point he began a peripatetic career in the theater, eventually finding his niche on Broadway as a light comedian. When he made his move to motion pictures—as one of dozens of stage stars being signed by movie studios of the day to lend legitimacy to the new feature-film form—Fairbanks was thirty-two years old, and his success was considered a bit of a long shot. He never quite fit in with D. W. Griffith's other theatrical imports at the Triangle/Fine Arts studio, but he received a solid grounding in filmmaking there; within eighteen months, he was working independently, and in 1919 he became a founding partner of United Artists. Working with such reliable talents as John Emerson, Anita Loos, Allan Dwan, and Victor Fleming, Fairbanks created the character of

"Doug," a breezy, all-American go-getter who seemed to move effortlessly through life and across the screen, surmounting every comic and dramatic difficulty with wit and grace. In 1920, with the release of *The Mark of Zorro*, Fairbanks moved into the production of costume films, averaging one a year for the rest of the decade. The advent of sound in film found him uncertain about which direction to take, and after several uninspired efforts, he retired from the screen in the early 1930s. He died in 1939.

Curator Iris Barry approached Fairbanks just before his death and asked him to consider depositing his work with The Museum of Modern Art for safekeeping. At the time, the actor/producer had film materials for approximately twenty of the independently produced films in his vaults, as well as numerous reels of home movies featuring himself and his wife, Mary Pickford, taken at Pickfair and on various trips abroad. The bulk of this footage arrived by ship in New York in 1938, and the making of

*(continued on page 92)*

Victor Fleming.
**The Mollycoddle**.
1920.
*Douglas Fairbanks
(center), Wallace
Beery (right)*

*The Mollycoddle*, Douglas Fairbanks's third
film for United Artists (which he
cofounded in 1919 with Mary Pickford,
Charles Chaplin, and D. W. Griffith) is
also one of Fairbanks's last films with a
contemporary setting, before he turned
full-time to the production of costume
subjects during the 1920s. In the film, he
plays a fifth-generation American who
lives in Europe and is so far removed
from the land of his forefathers that he
has become comically emasculated. On a
lark, he is shanghaied by a trio of young
Americans onto a yacht headed for the
U.S., only to discover that the captain is a
jewel smuggler on his way to the American Southwest. The silly plot serves
merely as a hook on which to hang some
of Fairbanks's most inventive visual gags
as well as a means of incorporating dramatic footage from the Navajo County
Hopi Indian Reservation. Logical narratives were never Fairbanks's strong suit,
and in *The Mollycoddle* he demonstrated
once again that his breathtaking physical
prowess and undaunted optimism could
overcome any obstacles.

Fred Niblo.
**The Mark of
Zorro**. 1920.
*Douglas Fairbanks,
Marguerite de la
Motte, Robert McKim*

Victor Fleming.
**When the Clouds Roll By**. 1919.
*Douglas Fairbanks, Herbert Grimwood*

Theodore Reed.
**The Nut**. 1921.
*Douglas Fairbanks*

(continued from page 90)
new prints of the most important works began almost immediately. In 1940 the Museum presented *The Career of the Late Douglas Fairbanks*, a landmark exhibition of his most significant films, accompanied by the publication of Alistair Cooke's *Douglas Fairbanks: The Making of a Screen Character*, a pioneering evaluation of the man, his persona, and his work. Over the years, this original donation to the Museum's permanent film collection has been the basis for countless exhibitions, both here and around the world, resulting in ongoing appreciation for and study of Fairbanks's unique contributions to film culture.

Fred Niblo.
**The Three Musketeers**.
1921. *Leon Barry, Eugene Pallette, Douglas Fairbanks, George Siegmann*

Allan Dwan.
**Robin Hood**. 1923.
*Douglas Fairbanks,*
*Enid Bennett*

Donald Crisp. **Don Q, Son of Zorro**. 1925. *Douglas Fairbanks*

Portraying both father and son, Douglas Fairbanks filled this simple tale of homecoming with all the elements of swashbuckling adventure and physical peril for which he is justly famous. A somewhat slower and more stately film than its predecessor, *The Mark of Zorro* (1920), *Don Q, Son of Zorro* nevertheless achieves a level of grandeur missing in the earlier effort, due in large part to its richly detailed set design and Fairbanks's self-confident and generous spirit. In every one of his costume films, Fairbanks demonstrates a newly learned physical trick or feat of daring, and *Don Q* is no exception; here, he reveals with great precision and elegance his recently acquired dexterity with whips, a talent of little practical use in most everyday life, but one which nevertheless impressed audiences and colleagues alike.

Raoul Walsh.
**The Thief of Bagdad**. 1924. *Anna May Wong (standing), Douglas Fairbanks*

Albert Parker.
**The Black Pirate**. 1926. *Billie Dove, Douglas Fairbanks*

Allan Dwan.
**The Iron Mask**.
1929. *Leon Barry,
Gino Corrado,
Stanley J. Sandford,
Douglas Fairbanks,
Nigel de Brulier*

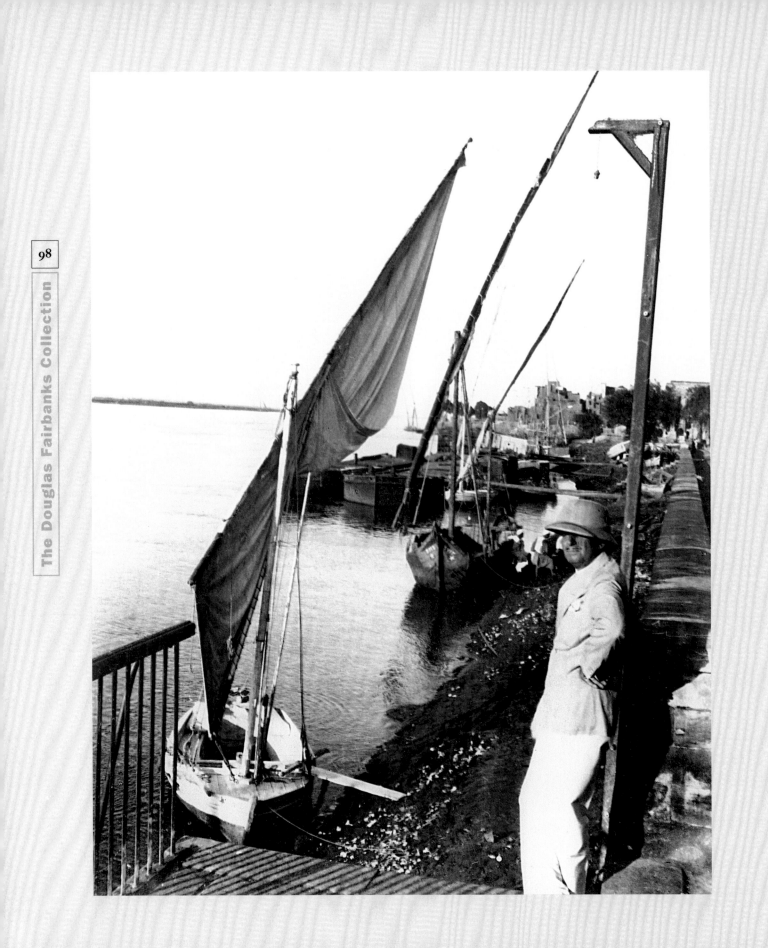

*Opposite:*
Victor Fleming and
Douglas Fairbanks.
**Around the World
in Eighty Minutes
with Douglas
Fairbanks**. 1931.
*Douglas Fairbanks*

The Fairbanks
Collection arriving
in New York from
California by
boat, 1940.

John Ford.
**The Iron Horse**.
1924

With *The Iron Horse*, director John Ford returned to his early film roots to make a Western, but one of epic size and scope. The heroic tale of the building of the first transcontinental railroad provides the historical backdrop for the story of Davy Brandon, a young surveyor for the Union Pacific, whose father had been murdered many years before while pursuing his own dream of a rail link between the East and the West. Character and landscape inform and subtly reflect one another as the story moves relentlessly toward the driving of the final spike near Promontory, Utah, in 1869. Ford foregrounds the ethnic diversity of the gangs that worked on the monumental project—giving pride of place, as always, to his beloved Irish—and shows how, in the face of adversity, the workers were able to overcome their differences and work together, becoming, in the process, a microcosm of the national ideal.

*Opposite:*
Yakov Protazanov.
**Aelita**. 1924

*Above:*
F. W. Murnau.
**Der letzte Mann
(The Last Laugh)**.
1924. *Emil Jannings*

*Right:*
Ernst Lubitsch.
**The Marriage
Circle**. 1924.
*Marie Prevost,
Monte Blue*

*Opposite:*
Fernand Léger.
**Ballet mécanique**.
1924

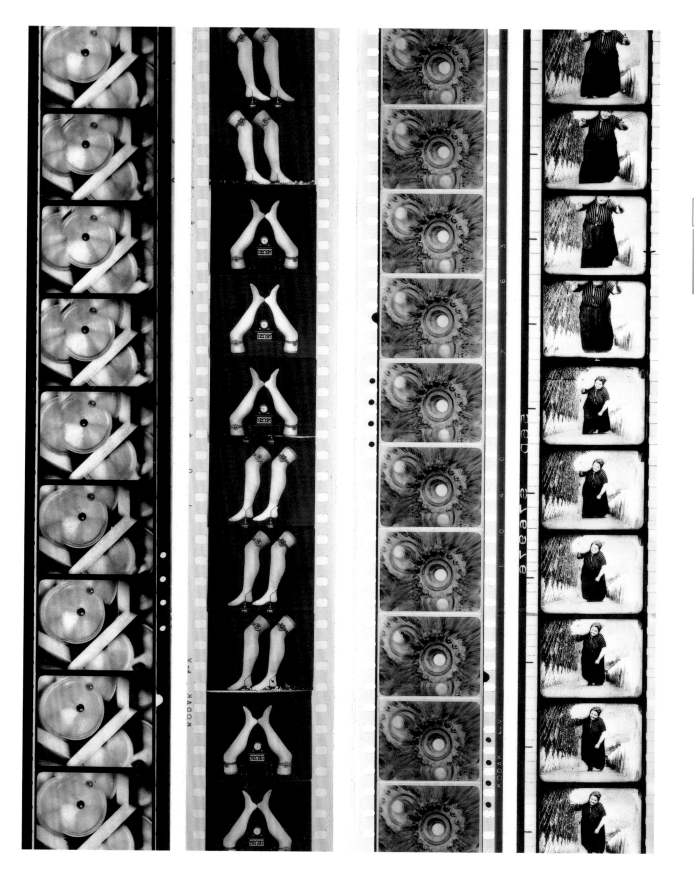

*Opposite:*
Marcel L'Herbier.
**L'Inhumaine.** 1924

René Clair.
**Entr'acte.** 1924

A classic of avant-garde cinema, *Entr'acte* was made as an intermission piece for the Ballets Suédois production of *Relâche*, a Dada theater work that premiered in Paris in December of 1924. The ballet's director, Francis Picabia, gave René Clair a short scenario around which to build the film, and Erik Satie composed an original score to accompany it, but the finished work is "pure" cinema—the individual shots and the connections between them resulting in what Clair described as "visual babblings." Key figures of the contemporary Parisian art world appear in the film in absurd comic cameos, including Man Ray, Marcel Duchamp, Jean Borlin (director of the Ballets Suédois), Georges Auric, Picabia, and Clair himself. As Picabia declared, *Entr'acte* "respects nothing except the right to roar with laughter."

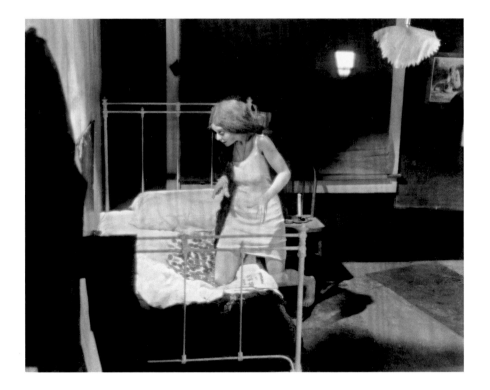

Erich von Stroheim.
**Greed**. 1925.
*ZaSu Pitts*

Charles Chaplin.
**The Gold Rush**.
1925. *Charles Chaplin,
Georgia Hale*

Lynn Reynolds.
**Riders of the
Purple Sage**. 1925.
*Marion Nixon*

G. W. Pabst.
**Die freudlose
Gasse (The Joyless
Street)**. 1925.
*Greta Garbo (far
right)*

Dmitri Kirsanov.
**Ménilmontant**.
1925.
*Nadia Sibirskaya*

109

1920s

King Vidor.
**The Big Parade**.
1925. *Renée Adorée,*
*John Gilbert*

Frank Borzage.
**Lazybones**. 1925.
*Charles "Buck" Jones*

Herbert Brenon.
**A Kiss for
Cinderella**. 1925.
*Betty Bronson,
Tom Moore*

On the heels of director Herbert Brenon's successful 1924 adaptation of James M. Barrie's stage hit *Peter Pan*, Paramount Pictures quickly put into production another Barrie property, *A Kiss for Cinderella*, again with Brenon at the helm. In this fantasy, Betty Bronson (who portrayed Peter in the earlier film) plays Cinderella, a servant girl in wartime London who still believes in fairies. Suspected of aiding the enemy, she is cleared of all suspicion with the help of an artist, for whom she works, and a young policeman. One day, she falls asleep at the snow-covered threshold of her lodgings with four caged mice and a pumpkin, and dreams that she is Cinderella from the fairy tale. After waking from her magical sleep, she finds herself in the young policeman's arms, her dream now a reality. A whimsical, timeless fantasy, *A Kiss for Cinderella* also contains elements that satirize the foibles of the modern world. In the end, it is Bronson's moving performance in the title role that carries this film right through to its final fade-out, one that rivals the ending of Charles Chaplin's *City Lights* (1931) in sadness and beauty.

*Right:*
Henrik Galeen.
**Der Student von Prag (The Student of Prague)**.
1926. *Conrad Veidt*

*Below, left:*
Jean Renoir.
**Nana**. 1926.
*Jean Angelo,
Catherine Hessling*

*Below, right:*
Alfred E. Green.
**Ella Cinders**.
1926. *Colleen Moore*

Marcel Duchamp.
**Anemic Cinema**.
1926

Robert J. Flaherty.
**Moana**. 1926

Fritz Lang.
**Metropolis**. 1927.
*Brigitte Helm*

"An exaggerated dream of the New York skyline, multiplied a thousandfold and divested of all reality," is film critic Lotte Eisner's apt description of the Expressionist cityscape created by Lang and his team for *Metropolis*, about a dystopian city of the future where the working masses live underground, enslaved by the wealthy few. When Fredersen, the Master of Metropolis, fears a revolt among the workers, he enlists the aid of a scientist to create a robot built in the image of Maria, a young woman whose rhetoric has inspired the downtrodden to turn on the elite class. In the end, disaster is averted and all are reconciled, a trite finale that undercuts much of what precedes it (Lang himself claimed to have "detested" the final product). But the visual daring of *Metropolis* pays tribute to Lang's architectural training, and his masterful choreography of crowds and machinery creates a kind of visualized sound rarely before seen in cinema.

Man Ray.
**Emak Bakia**. 1926

Vsevolod Pudovkin.
**Mat' (Mother)**.
1926.
*Vera Baranovskaya,*
*Nikolai Batalov*

International Workers
Aid. **Passaic Textile
Strike**. 1926

On January 25, 1926, pushed to the point
of desperation by wage cuts, lengthened
hours, and unsafe work conditions, the
largely immigrant workforce in the textile
mills of Passaic, New Jersey, shut down
their city's textile industry for over a year.
Although the strikers at first hired professional filmmakers to cover the event, they
were forced to finish the job themselves
when the original crew eventually bowed
out, declaring the filming conditions
unsafe. The result is a landmark in the
history of the documentary genre. The
film opens with a prologue that tells the
story of a representative family and its
experience in the mills, and continues
with the unfolding of the strike and the
formation of a union. Some of the events
depicted are reenactments, and the strike
was still unresolved when the film was
completed; yet *Passaic Textile Strike* was a
resounding success, raising money for the
International Workers Aid and spreading
the gospel of labor solidarity nationwide.

F. W. Murnau.
**Faust**. 1926.
*Gösta Ekmann,
Camilla Horn*

Dave Fleischer.
**Inklings, Issue 12**.
1927

Buster Keaton and
Clyde Bruckman.
**The General**.
1927. *Buster Keaton*

Merian C. Cooper
and Ernest B.
Schoedsack.
**Chang**. 1927

Allan Dwan.
**East Side, West
Side**. 1927.
*George O'Brien*

William A. Wellman.
**Wings**. 1927

Mauritz Stiller.
**Hotel Imperial**.
1927. *Pola Negri,*
*Max Davidson*

Clarence G. Badger.
**It**. 1927. *Clara Bow*
*(right)*

Alan Crosland.
**The Jazz Singer**.
1927. *Al Jolson*

*The Jazz Singer* is widely believed to be the first sound film, despite clear and overwhelming evidence to the contrary; it was, however, the first film with a synchronized music and vocal track to truly capture the public imagination, ushering in the sound revolution. The story is a fairly trite melodrama concerning a young Jewish man who wishes to sing popular music but who, in so doing, incurs the wrath of his father, a respected cantor. Essentially a silent film with a prerecorded musical score, *The Jazz Singer* comes briefly to life in those moments when its star, Al Jolson, ad-libs dialogue, most notably in the scene where he sits at an upright piano in the family parlor and talks gently to his mother. The intimacy of their relationship comes through loud and clear, sounding the death knell of the silent film. Even though the following year, 1928, would be considered by many to be one of the golden years of silent cinema, by 1929 Hollywood had converted almost exclusively to talkies.

*Opposite:*
F. W. Murnau.
**Sunrise: A Song of
Two Humans**.
1927. *Janet Gaynor,
George O'Brien*

*Above:*
Robert Florey.
**The Life and
Death of 9413—A
Hollywood Extra**.
1928. *Raucourt*

*Above:*
Karl Brown. **Stark
Love**. 1927. *Forrest
James, Helen Munday*

*Left:*
Esther Shub.
**Padeniye dinasti
Romanovikh (Fall
of the Romanov
Dynasty)**. 1927

Carl Theodor Dreyer.
**La Passion de
Jeanne d'Arc (The
Passion of Joan of
Arc).** 1928.
*Renée Falconetti*

Frank Borzage.
**Seventh Heaven.**
1927. *Charles Farrell,
Janet Gaynor*

John Ford.
**Hangman's House**.
1928. *Larry Kent,*
*June Collyer, Victor*
*McLaglen*

Luis Buñuel and
Salvador Dalí.
**Un Chien
Andalou**. 1928

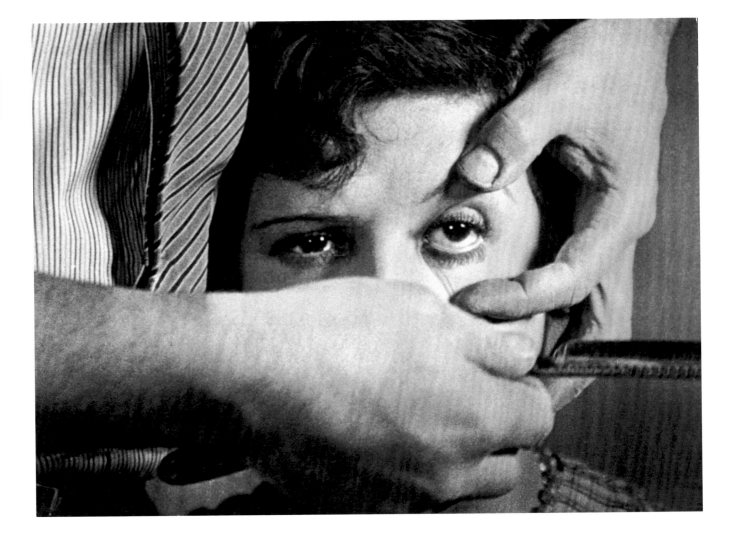

*Above, left:*
W. S. Van Dyke.
**White Shadows in
the South Seas**.
1928. *Monte Blue*

*Above, right:*
Hans Richter.
**Vormittagsspuk
(Ghosts Before
Breakfast)**. 1928

*Right:*
Josef von
Sternberg.
**The Docks of
New York**. 1928.
*George Bancroft
(right)*

Jean Epstein.
**La Chute de la
maison Usher
(The Fall of the
House of Usher).**
1928

A leading member of the French cinema's avant-garde movement and the director of the Impressionist classic *Coeur fidèle* (1923), Jean Epstein broke with his more modernist colleagues in the late 1920s to make documentaries and fiction films grounded in the realities of everyday life. Before that evolution, however, Epstein filmed this adaptation of two Edgar Allan Poe stories: "The Fall of the House of Usher" (1839) and "The Oval Portrait" (1850). The film's significance lies not so much in its fidelity to Poe's stories as in its atmospheric evocation of the author's gothic sensibility. Misty, fog-shrouded scenes, slow-motion photography, markedly low camera angles, unhurried panning and tracking shots, intricate lighting, and numerous other camera tricks lend themselves to eerie supernatural effects. "Since the French Impressionist school has always considered the cinema to be like a visual symphony, we might call this film by Epstein the cinematic equivalent of Debussy's works," observed Henri Langlois, film historian and founder of the Cinemathèque Française, in Paris. "The actors were merely objects."

*Opposite:*
Frank Borzage.
**Street Angel.** 1928.
*Charles Farrell,
Janet Gaynor*

Jean Renoir.
**La Petite
Marchande
d'allumettes (The
Little Match Girl)**.
1928. *Manuel Raaby,
Catherine Hessling*

Victor Sjöström.
**The Wind**. 1928.
*Lillian Gish*

Paul Leni.
**The Man Who**
**Laughs**. 1928.
*Conrad Veidt,*
*Mary Philbin*

Josef von Sternberg.
**The Last Command**.
1928. *Emil Jannings*

Sergei Eisenstein.
**Oktyabr' (October;
Ten Days That
Shook the World)**.
1928. *Nikandrovi
(as Lenin)*

*Opposite:*
Anthony Asquith.
**Underground**.
1928. *Elissa Landi,
Cyril McLaglen*

In this, Anthony Asquith's second feature
film, two men compete for the affection
of a beautiful shopgirl, their rivalry
culminating in tragedy atop London's
Battersea Power Station. *Underground*
possesses the narrative self-assurance and
visual sophistication of many late silent
films, yet the fact that its director and
writer was only twenty-six years old at the
time makes the accomplishment remarkable.
The film startled British audiences with
its setting of a working-class love story in
an ultramodern London landscape and its
deeply shadowed, German-influenced
lighting schemes.

*Below:*
Marcel L'Herbier.
**L'Argent**. 1929.
*Brigitte Helm*

A French and German coproduction based on the 1891 novel by Émile Zola, *L'Argent* tells the story of Saccard, a financier who plans to boost the price of his faltering stock by enlisting the aviator Hamelin in a publicity stunt involving flying across the Atlantic to drill for oil. When Saccard attempts to seduce Hamelin's wife, she realizes that the tycoon is not what he seems and exposes him to the financial world as a fraud. The film theorist Noël Burch declared *L'Argent* the first film "to systematically use camera movement to establish the basic rhythm of the film's *découpage*, thereby anticipating by twenty years [Orson] Welles's and [Michelangelo] Antonioni's film styles at their most sophisticated." In addition to constantly shifting the camera's point of view, director Marcel L'Herbier used enormous sets to dwarf his characters, whose crazed pursuit of money is made to seem inconsequential by comparison. Once derided as merely an overlong and expensive failure (at its premiere it ran to nearly three hours), *L'Argent* is now viewed by film critics and historians as perhaps the finest synthesis of the avant-garde and commercial cinema ever produced.

*Opposite:*
Alfred Hitchcock.
**Blackmail**. 1929.
*Anny Ondra*

Ted Wilde.
**Speedy.** 1928.
*Ann Christy,*
*Harold Lloyd*

**139**

**1920s**

Dziga Vertov.
**Chelovek s
kinoapparatom
(The Man with the
Movie Camera).**
1929

Murray Roth.
**Lambchops**. 1929.
*George Burns,*
*Gracie Allen*

Rouben Mamoulian.
**Applause**. 1929.
*Helen Morgan (right)*

James W. Horne.
**Big Business**.
1929. *Stan Laurel,
Oliver Hardy*

141

1920s

Ernst Lubitsch.
**The Love Parade**.
1929. *Jeannette
MacDonald, Maurice
Chevalier*

Ralph Steiner.
**H₂O**. 1929

Joris Ivens.
**Regen (Rain)**.
1929

# 1930s

*Opposite:*
Josef von Sternberg.
**Der blaue Engel
(The Blue Angel)**.
1930.
*Marlene Dietrich*

Raoul Walsh.
**The Big Trail**.
1930. *Marguerite
Churchill, John
Wayne*

Filmed simultaneously in both standard 35mm and Grandeur, an early wide-screen process, and with versions shot in German, Italian, French, and Spanish for foreign markets (in standard 35mm only and with alternate casts), this 1930 sound feature by veteran silent director Raoul Walsh is an impressive epic of the Oregon Trail. Although hampered by difficult locations and the new and unwieldy Grandeur apparatus, cinematographer Arthur Edeson succeeded in filling the screen with breathtaking natural vistas as well as beautifully composed close-ups of the young stars, Marguerite Churchill and John Wayne (in his first starring role). Moments of low comedy are woven awkwardly into the narrative, but the overall effect is one of high drama. The Museum of Modern Art spent many years on the preservation of this film, working with original elements in its Fox Collection; the result is the first restoration of the complete 70mm wide-screen Grandeur version, copied to anamorphic 35mm.

Josef von Sternberg.
**Morocco**. 1930.
*Marlene Dietrich,*
*Gary Cooper*

Alexander Dovzhenko.
**Zemlya (Earth)**.
1930

John Ford.
**Up the River**. 1930.
*Spencer Tracy (seated at left)*

René Clair.
**Sous les toits de Paris (Under the Roofs of Paris)**. 1930

Mikhail Kalatozov.
**Sol Svanetii (Salt
for Svanetia).** 1930

Ralph Steiner.
**Mechanical
Principles**. 1930

Luis Buñuel.
**L'Age d'or**. 1930.
*Lya Lys*

This Surrealist masterpiece opens with documentary footage of scorpions doing battle, followed by a series of events staged on a seacoast, including the interruption of partisans by a procession of chanting clerics and the arrival of a group of dignitaries in formal dress, intent on founding the Roman Empire. This last ceremony is brought to a scandalized halt by the appearance of a pair of passionate (and quite vocal) lovers writhing in the mud nearby. The film continues in this spirit for an hour, employing the music of Beethoven, Mozart, Mendelssohn, Debussy, and Wagner as a kind of connective tissue for, and aural commentary on, the unnerving visuals. In the end, the lovers are doomed to frustration, as institutions of authority (the clergy, army, police, and bourgeois society) impede their attempts at consummation. *L'Age d'or* provoked riots when it premiered in Paris in December of 1930, and within two weeks of its opening it was banned by French authorities for its blasphemy and subversive worldview.

Left:
Dziga Vertov.
**Entuziazm
(Enthusiasm).**
1931

Opposite:
Fritz Lang.
**M.** 1931

Jay Leyda.
**A Bronx Morning**.
1931

Ralph Steiner.
**Surf and Seaweed**.
1931

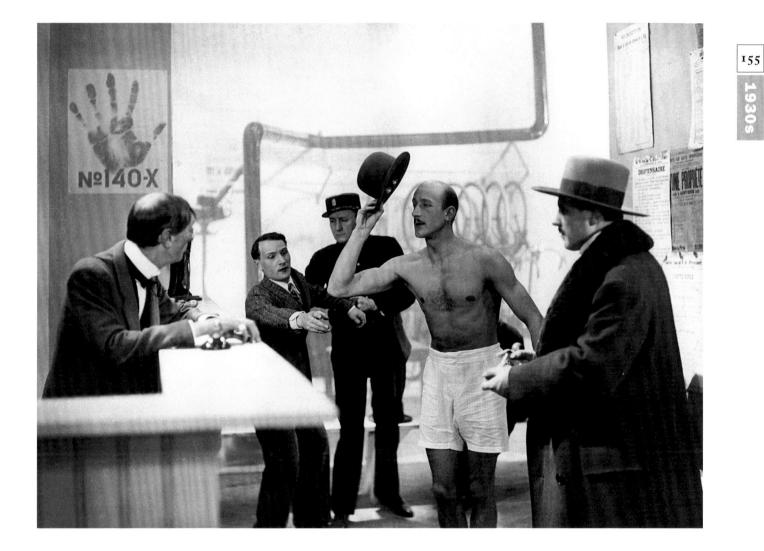

Sergei Eisenstein.
**¡Que viva Mexico!**
1931. Unedited
footage

*Opposite:*
F. W. Murnau.
**Tabu.** 1931

George Cukor.
**A Bill of Divorce-ment**. 1932.
*Katharine Hepburn,
John Barrymore*

Frank Capra.
**American Madness**. 1932.
*Walter Huston*

Ernst Lubitsch.
**Trouble in Paradise**. 1932.
*Miriam Hopkins,
Herbert Marshall*

In a letter to critic Herman Weinberg, Ernst Lubitsch once wrote, "As for pure style I think I have done nothing better or good as *Trouble in Paradise*." Admittedly, the plot is flimsy: Two jewel thieves (Gaston and Lily) meet and fall in love. They plan to rob a rich widow, but once Gaston insinuates himself into the widow's household and business affairs, Lily suspects that he may have designs on more than her money. The entire plan is revealed, Gaston is allowed to escape, and

he and Lily are reconciled. What at first seem little more than discrete episodes, however, are skillfully linked—by the consistent employment of fluid camera movements and subtle visual effects; urbane, nonstop dialogue (adapted by Samson Raphaelson from a Hungarian farce by Laszlo Aladar); and musical score by W. Franke Harling, which comments wittily and continuously on (and beneath) the action.

Max Ophuls.
**Liebelei**. 1932.
*Magda Schneider,
Luise Ullrich*

William Dieterle.
**Adorable**. 1933.
*Henry Garat,
Janet Gaynor*

Joris Ivens.
**Borinage**. 1933

Lewis Milestone.
**Hallelujah I'm a
Bum**. 1933. *Al Jolson,
Harry Langdon*

Leo McCarey.
**Duck Soup**. 1933.
*Groucho Marx*

The Marx Brothers (Groucho, Chico, Harpo, and Zeppo) were products of the rough-and-tumble world of vaudeville, in which performers tested and refined stage routines over the course of many years, before audiences in theaters big and small across America. By the time they had been signed to the movies in 1929, they were established stars, appearing nightly on Broadway. Yet they never lost their hard-won love of anarchy nor their predilection for satirizing all forms of authority and pomposity. Their first four films for Paramount more or less duplicated the formula that had served them so well on the stage, one in which their unorthodox routines were tempered by traditional musical comedy stage business involving juveniles, ingenues, and romantic subplots. In *Duck Soup* this formula was dropped altogether, and the result is pure, unadulterated Marx Brothers. As always, they revel in physical slapstick as well as the verbal fireworks (chief among them double entendres, non sequiturs, and puns) that had become their trademark, but now they were free to follow their comedic instincts with abandon. The public received the final product with bewilderment, the box office was dismal, and the brothers were dropped by Paramount. Soon after, they signed with MGM, where producer Irving Thalberg smoothed over their rough edges and made them popular again.

Dudley Murphy.
**The Emperor
Jones**. 1933.
*Paul Robeson,
Dudley Digges*

Frank Capra.
**It Happened One
Night**. 1934.
*Claudette Colbert,
Clark Gable*

*Opposite:*
Robert J. Flaherty.
**Man of Aran**. 1934.
*Maggie Dirrance*

*Below:*
Leni Riefenstahl.
**Der Triumph des
Willens (Triumph
of the Will)**. 1936

Mario Camerini.
**Darò un milione**.
1935. *Assia Noris*

*Opposite:*
George Stevens.
**Swing Time**. 1936.
*Ginger Rogers,
Fred Astaire*

George Stevens started in the movie business and worked throughout the 1920s as a cameraman. In 1927 he joined Hal Roach's studio, where he shot many of Laurel and Hardy's best short films, among them *Two Tars* (1928), *Big Business* (1929), and *Hog Wild* (1930). By 1933 he had moved to RKO and graduated to feature directing. RKO's biggest box office stars in the mid-1930s were Fred Astaire and Ginger Rogers, and although Stevens was not a director of musicals, he had garnered enough critical and popular success with his film of the previous year, *Alice Adams* (1935), that he won with the director's

chair on the pair's sixth release. *Swing Time* centers on the on-again, off-again relationship between Lucky (Astaire), a small-time hoofer and sometime gambler, and Penny (Rogers), a hard-working dance instructor—roles that allowed the team plenty of opportunities for their iconographic dancing. Years of experience in two-reel comedies allowed Stevens to draw fine performances from veteran supporting players Victor Moore and Helen Broderick, and the score by Jerome Kern and Dorothy Fields provided the perfect setting for some of Astaire and Hermes Pan's most memorable choreography.

Pare Lorentz.
**The Plow That
Broke the Plains**.
1936

Fritz Lang.
**You Only Live
Once**. 1937.
*Sylvia Sidney*

Pare Lorentz.
**The River**. 1937

Written and directed by Pare Lorentz for the U.S. Farm Security Administration, *The River* is a follow-up to Lorentz's groundbreaking documentary of the previous year, *The Plow That Broke the Plains* (1936). As with the earlier film, Lorentz sought out the finest cameramen working in documentary filmmaking—in this case hiring Willard Van Dyke, Floyd Crosby, and Horace and Stacey Woodard—and brought back composer Virgil Thomson to write and score the music. Unlike the first film, however, *The River* was fully funded and promoted by the Roosevelt administration, and it achieved wide distribution through Paramount. Striking photography and rhythmically insistent editing tell the story of the Mississippi River and its tributaries, their tendency to flood their banks regularly and with great destructive force, and the American grit and ingenuity that tamed the river valley and turned it into a productive, power-generating landscape. *The River* suffers from a weak, if hopeful, finale—as with all such stories, the problem is more dramatic and visually arresting than the solution. But at its best, Lorentz's film became a model for the new documentary cinema of social advocacy.

*Above, left:*
Kenji Mizoguchi.
**Gion no shimai
(Sisters of the
Gion).** 1936.
*Isuzu Yamada*

*Above, right:*
Sidney Meyers
and Jay Leyda.
**People of the
Cumberland.**
1937

*Left:*
Jean Renoir.
**La Grande
Illusion (Grand
Illusion).** 1937.
*Erich von Stroheim,
Pierre Fresnay,
Jean Gabin*

Joris Ivens.
**The Spanish
Earth**. 1937

Sergei Eisenstein.
**Alexander
Nevsky**. 1938

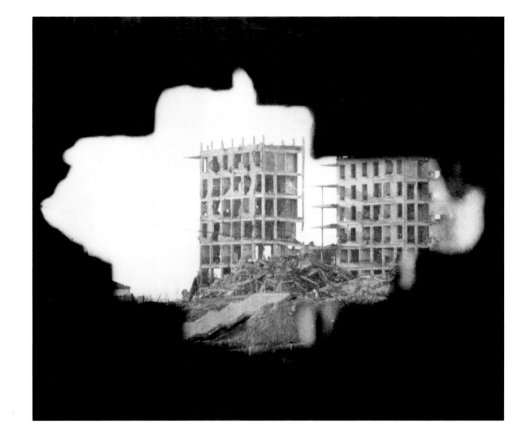

Michael Curtiz and
William Keighley.
**The Adventures
of Robin Hood**.
1938. *Basil Rathbone,
Errol Flynn*

Had he never made another film, Errol
Flynn would still be remembered today
for his spirited, pitch-perfect performance
in Michael Curtiz and William Keighley's
*The Adventures of Robin Hood*. As critic
David Thomson has written, "Flynn does
not deal in depth, but he has a freshness, a
galvanizing energy, a cheerful gaiety (in
the old sense) made to inspire boys." It
was Curtiz who took Flynn and molded
him into a swashbuckler; the two worked
together on eleven films between 1935
and 1941, virtually all of which cast the
star as a suave and fearless action hero.
These are the roles for which Flynn is

best remembered, and none is as near
flawless as his Robin of Locksley. With
Olivia de Haviland as Maid Marian (the
third of her seven films with Flynn), glori-
ous Technicolor photography by Tony
Gaudio, Sol Polito, and W. Howard
Green, a stirring musical score by Erich
Wolfgang Korngold, and performances by
some of Hollywood's finest supporting
players—including Basil Rathbone, Claude
Rains, Patric Knowles, Alan Hale, Eugene
Pallette, and Una O'Connor, *The Adventures
of Robin Hood* survives as one of the finest
examples of pure entertainment to emerge
from the Hollywood studio system.

Howard Hawks.
**Bringing Up
Baby**. 1938. *Cary
Grant, Katharine
Hepburn, Walter
Catlett, Fritz Feld
(far right)*

Henri Cartier-
Bresson.
**Return to Life**.
1938

*Opposite:*
Marcel Carné.
**Quai des brumes
(Port of Shadows)**.
1938. *Jean Gabin,
Michèle Morgan*

Marcel **Carné** was a veteran of the French
film industry when he directed his first
film in 1936 (*Jenny*). Two years later he
made *Quai des brumes*, a profoundly pes-
simistic yet highly successful film that
benefited from the contributions of such
major talents as Jacques Prévert (screenplay), Eugen Schüfftan (cinematography),
Coco Chanel (costumes), and Maurice
Jaubert (music). This film was followed
by *Hôtel du Nord* (1938), *Le Jour se lève*
(1939), and *Les Enfants du paradis* (1944),
all of which were released to great critical
and popular acclaim, establishing Carné
as the most successful French filmmaker
of the era. Each of these films showed
Carné to be canny in his choice of collab-
orators while also playing to his personal
strengths of technical virtuosity, visual
sophistication, and melancholy mise-en-
scène. *Quai des brumes* in particular
exhibits the last of these traits, relating
the story of an army deserter who arrives
in the port city of Le Havre in search of a
new life, only to discover an underworld
filled with lost souls, themselves in need
of salvation. Carné's subsequent work
showed a significant slackening of energy
and ambition, but the films of this period
stand as a ringing endorsement of the
collaborative nature of filmmaking.

Dudley Murphy.
**. . . One Third of a
Nation . . .** 1939

Lewis Milestone.
**Of Mice and Men**.
1939. *Lon Chaney, Jr.,*
*Burgess Meredith*

Leo McCarey.
**Love Affair**. 1939.
*Irene Dunne,*
*Charles Boyer*

*Above:*
Marcel Carné.
**Hôtel du Nord**.
1938. *Annabella*

*Above, right:*
John Cromwell.
**Made for Each
Other**. 1939.
*James Stewart,
Carole Lombard
(center)*

*Right:*
Ernst Lubitsch.
**Ninotchka**. 1939.
*Greta Garbo,
Alexander Granach,
Sig Rumann,
Felix Bressart*

Frank Capra.
**Mr. Smith Goes
to Washington**.
1939. *James Stewart*

Ralph Steiner and
Willard Van Dyke.
**The City**. 1939

John Ford.
**Stagecoach**. 1939

# 1940s

Herbert Kline.
**Lights Out in
Europe**. 1940

Howard Hawks.
**His Girl Friday**.
*1940. Rosalind
Russell, Cary Grant,
Billy Gilbert,
Clarence Kolb*

Fast and furiously funny, *His Girl Friday*
blends two formulas popular in Hollywood
movies of the late 1930s: biting political
satire and romantic screwball comedy. In
the film, Walter Burns, the managing editor of a city newspaper, ruthlessly scoops
the competition by hiding a death row
fugitive with his top reporter and writer,
Hildy Johnson—who also happens to be
his ex-wife. Although Walter and Hildy
clash professionally and romantically, it is
a given that he and the paper cannot get
along without her. Adding to the fun are
Johnson's fiancé, whose courting is
sweetly inept, and a messenger from the
state governor, whose rejection of a bribe
from the city's mayor is the film's
wickedest moment of truth. In *His Girl
Friday* nothing is allowed to interfere with
the dizzying pace set by the actors, who
compete to interrupt each other. The talk
crackles with wit; the overlapping dialogue of seasoned journalists and mayoral
henchmen is smart, real, and mean. It is
Hawksian comedy at its best—a battle of
the sexes with the roles reversed to allow
for plenty of humiliation and triumph on
both sides.

Preston Sturges.
**The Lady Eve**.
*1941. Henry Fonda,
Barbara Stanwyck*

John Ford.
**How Green Was
My Valley**. 1941.
*Anna Lee, Roddy
McDowall*

Orson Welles.
**Citizen Kane**.
1941. *Joseph Cotten,
Orson Welles,
Everett Sloane*

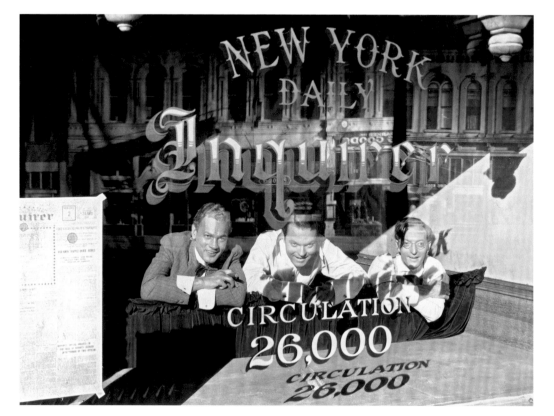

Jean Renoir.
**Swamp Water**.
1941. *Walter Huston,
Eugene Pallette, Anne
Baxter (fourth, fifth,
and sixth from left,
respectively)*

In 1939 Jean Renoir's *La Règle du jeu (The Rules of the Game)* opened in Paris to a storm of derision from critics and audiences alike. Criticized as both silly and unpatriotic, it was eventually denounced by the French government as "demoralizing," and banned. This personal trauma, combined with France's surrender to Hitler in 1940, led Renoir (and many other European filmmakers) to an unexpected exile in Hollywood. In 1941, Renoir signed a one-year contract with Darryl F. Zanuck's Twentieth Century–Fox studio, and after several false starts on other projects, he began production on a Dudley Nichols

script, *Swamp Water*. Renoir wanted to shoot most, if not all, of the film in Georgia's Okefenokee Swamp, where the story is set, but with the exception of several brief scenes shot on location without sound, Zanuck kept him tied to the studio backlot. Nevertheless, the final film possesses a visual authenticity and a striking empathy for its characters. As with all copies of *Swamp Water* distributed to theaters in 1941, The Museum of Modern Art's original release print is tinted sepia, an unusual, though canny, aesthetic choice that heightened the film's rustic sensibility.

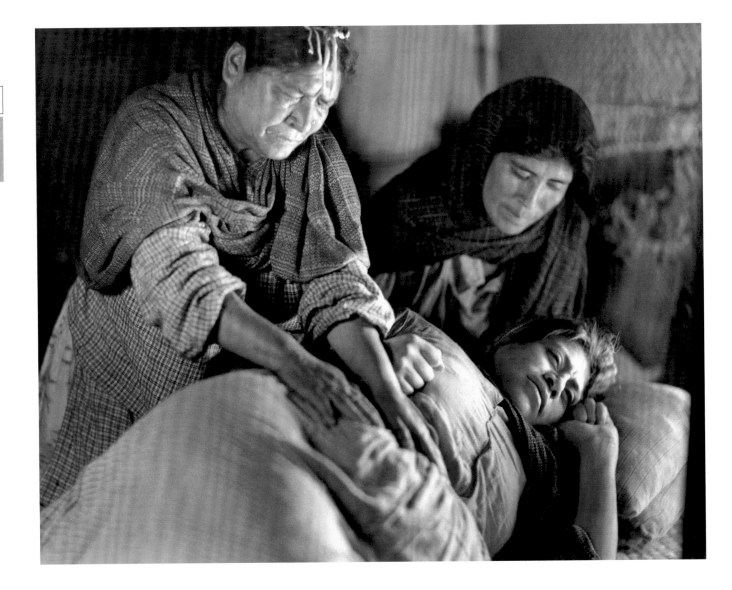

Herbert Kline.
**The Forgotten
Village**. 1941

John Huston.
**The Maltese
Falcon**. 1941.
*Humphrey Bogart,
Peter Lorre,
Mary Astor,
Sydney Greenstreet*

# The David O. Selznick Collection

The son of Lewis J. Selznick, an executive first at World Film and then at Selznick Pictures, David O. Selznick grew up surrounded by the movies. After working for his father's company as a youth, he moved briefly to MGM, and by his mid-twenties, he was a producer at Paramount. In 1931 he became the studio head at RKO and established strategic relationships with directors George Cukor (*What Price Hollywood?*, 1932, *A Bill of Divorcement*, 1932, *Little Women*, 1933), Gregory La Cava (*Symphony of Six Million*, 1932), and Merian C. Cooper and Ernest B. Schoedsack (*King Kong*, 1933). After returning to MGM in 1933 to head his own production unit, with which he turned out such hits as *Dinner at Eight* (George Cukor, 1933), *Manhattan Melodrama* (W. S. Van Dyke, 1934), *David Copperfield* (George Cukor, 1935), and *Anna Karenina* (Clarence Brown, 1935), he finally declared his independence with the formation of Selznick International Pictures in 1935. His partner was John Hay "Jock" Whitney, a venture capitalist, early investor in the three-strip Technicolor film process, and, no less importantly, the first chairman of The Museum of Modern Art's new Film Library Trustee Committee. For the new company, Selznick acted as president in charge of production on the West Coast, while Whitney served as chairman and East Coast manager.

Over the next fourteen years, Selznick produced an impressive roster of prestigious films primarily released through United Artists, including William Wellman's *A Star is Born*

William A. Wellman. **Nothing Sacred**. 1937. *Carole Lombard, Walter Connolly, Fredric March*

(1937) and *Nothing Sacred*; John Cromwell's *Made for Each Other* (1939); Gregory Ratoff's *Intermezzo* (1939); Alfred Hitchcock's *Rebecca* (1940), *Spellbound* (1945), and *The Paradine Case* (1947); King Vidor's *Duel in the Sun* (1946); and, most famously, Victor Fleming's *Gone with the Wind* (1939). Selznick's films reflect his obsession with detail at every level of production, as well as his penchant for acquiring and adapting proven literary properties. Critical opinion continues to be divided over his body of work, but no one has ever questioned the fact that, no matter who the director was, Selznick was the true author of the films that came out of his studio.

Upon his death in 1965, control of Selznick's films was assumed by his wife, Jennifer Jones, and then by ABC Pictures International, which donated all of the original film elements in the collection to the Museum in 1978. In the 1980s, the Museum undertook to preserve the entire collection, a major project, and when Walt Disney Pictures acquired ABC in the mid-1990s, it pursued its own preservation project, resulting in upgraded material donated to the film archive.

David O. Selznick,
John Hay Whitney,
and Merian C.
Cooper, c. 1939.

King Vidor.
**Duel in the Sun**.
1946. *Gregory Peck,
Jennifer Jones*

Alfred Hitchcock.
**Rebecca**. 1940.
*Joan Fontaine,
Judith Anderson*

Alfred Hitchcock.
**Suspicion.** 1941.
*Cary Grant,*
*Joan Fontaine*

Alfred Hitchcock.
**The Paradine
Case**. 1948.
*Gregory Peck (on the
witness stand)*

Michael Curtiz.
**Yankee Doodle
Dandy**. 1942.
*James Cagney*

Robert J. Flaherty.
**The Land**. 1942

Jacques Tourneur.
**Cat People**. 1942.
*Simone Simon*

Val Lewton was already a published author of fiction, nonfiction, and poetry when he began his film career as a publicity writer for MGM in 1928. In the mid-1930s, he took the job of story editor and assistant to producer David O. Selznick, then left MGM in 1942 when RKO offered him his own unit to produce low-budget horror films. At the time, RKO was in dire financial straits and hoped that a series of cheaply made films would turn a quick profit and keep the studio afloat. Lewton's first film, *Cat People*, did just that, earning several million dollars (estimates vary between $2 and $4 million) against a production cost of just under $135,000. Director Jacques Tourneur worked closely with Lewton to overcome the possible objections of industry censors by creating a sense of terror through the implied threat of violence, as well as keeping costs down by using expressive (and inexpensive) lighting techniques and oblique camera angles to compensate for their minuscule budget. The pair worked so efficiently that, by the time the box office returns had been reported for *Cat People*, they had already completed the second film in the series (*I Walked with a Zombie*, 1943), and were virtually finished with the third (*The Leopard Man*, 1943).

Anatole Litvak.
**The Battle of
Russia (Why We
Fight, no. 5).** 1943

Anthony Veiller.
**The Battle of
Britain (Why We
Fight, no. 4).** 1943

Michael Powell
and Emeric
Pressburger.
**The Life and
Death of Colonel
Blimp**. 1943. *Anton
Walbrook, Deborah
Kerr, Roger Livesey*

The tide of war was just beginning to turn in the Allies' favor when, in June of 1943, Michael Powell and Emeric Pressburger released *The Life and Death of Colonel Blimp*. But the English home front was still in jeopardy, and spirits were low. Just what was it that made England and its inhabitants special—and was it something that could be called upon to beat back the Nazis after nearly four years of bombardment and privation? Powell and Pressburger, equal partners in a company called The Archers, looked for answers to these questions in the person of Clive Wynne Candy, a fictional officer in the British army whose military career and personal life are traced over the course of half a century. Roger Livesey perfectly captures the bluster and naïveté of Candy as he ages from a dashing young officer to a bloated and blinkered old veteran. Throughout, the basic decency and integrity of England are contrasted with the ruthless militarism of Germany, leaving little doubt as to which nation was deserving of ultimate victory.

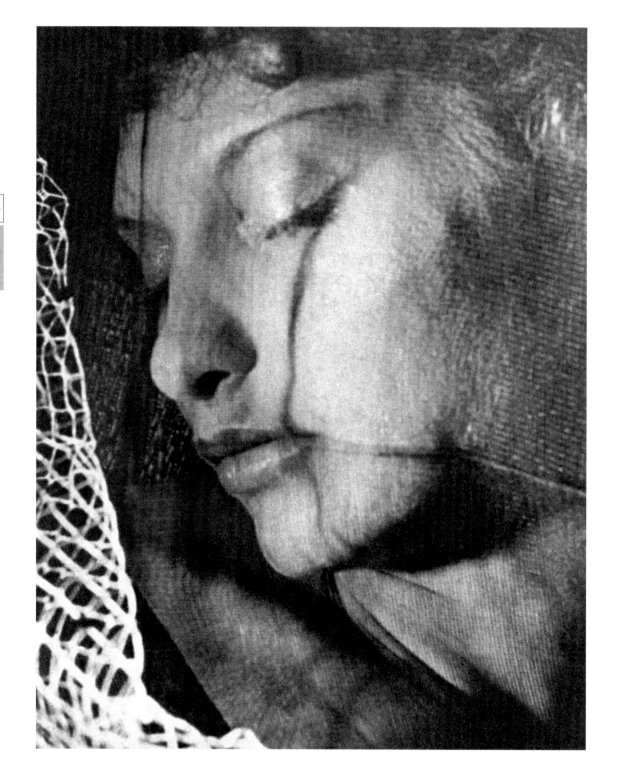

Maya Deren.
**Meshes of the
Afternoon**. 1943.
*Maya Deren*

Vincente Minnelli.
**Meet Me in
St. Louis**. 1944.
*Tom Drake,
Judy Garland*

Otto Preminger.
**Laura**. 1944.
*Gene Tierney,
Clifton Webb*

Maya Deren.
**At Land**. 1944.
*Maya Deren*

Maya Deren. **Study
in Choreography
for Camera**. 1945.
*Talley Beatty*

Upon their appearance in the mid-1940s, Maya Deren's films were described by *New York Times* dance critic John Martin as "choreocinema," a happy neologism that attempted to account for two of Deren's thematic preoccupations: the human body in motion and the filmmaking process itself. Her first two films, *Meshes of the Afternoon* (1943) and *At Land* (1944), began this endeavor (if only partially), but it was in her third project, *Study in Choreography for Camera*, that Deren fully realized her vision of freeing the human body from the confines of theatrical—and actual—space. In *Study*, a dancer (Talley Beatty) moves effortlessly within and between different environments (forest, living room, museum gallery, etc.), an achievement arrived at through the careful matching of his precisely choreographed movements with the film's editing pattern. As Beatty leaps from space to space across Deren's film splices, a new geographical reality is created, one where great distances can be covered within the span of just four minutes. Beatty's disciplined performance never betrays the difficulties that he and his director must have overcome to attain so fluid a result. Deren's camera, in effect, becomes Beatty's partner.

René Clément.
**Bataille du rail
(Battle of the
Rails)**. 1945

Michael Curtiz.
**Mildred Pierce**.
1945. *Joan Crawford,
Ann Blyth, Eve Arden*

*Left:*
Hans Richter.
**Dreams That
Money Can Buy**.
1946

*Below:*
Sergei Eisenstein.
**Ivan Grozny (Ivan
the Terrible)**. 1945.
*Nikolai Cherkasov*

*Below, left:*
William Wyler. **The
Best Years of Our
Lives**. 1946. *Dana
Andrews (in phone
booth), Hoagy
Carmichael, Harold
Russell, Fredric March*

201

1940s

Jean Cocteau.
**La Belle et la bête
(Beauty and the
Beast)**. 1946.
*Josette Day,
Jean Marais*

Roberto Rossellini.
**Paisà**. 1946.
*Alfonsino Pasca,
Dots M. Johnson*

Over fifteen years separate the making of
Jean Cocteau's first film, *Le Sang d'un
poète* (1930), and his second, *La Belle et la
bête*, yet the poetic sensibility and Surrealist imagery that animated the former is
still evident in the latter, though now in
the service of a more traditional narrative.
Never one for filming his fantasies in soft
focus, Cocteau understood that only
clean, unadorned photography could
properly convey the sense of mystery he
was after, making the on-screen world
that much more immediate and believ-
able. Beauty's home is lit and photographed as though it were a Vermeer
painting, and the Beast's castle, although
filled with living sculpture and darkened
hallways, is presented just as naturalisti-
cally. In an inspired twist on conventional
storytelling, Cocteau makes the viewer
long for the return of the Beast. Again, he
accomplished this feat through lenses and
lighting: "I persuaded my cameraman
[Henri] Alekan to shoot Jean Marais, as
the Prince, in as saccharine a style as possible. The trick worked. When the picture
was released, letters poured in from matrons,
teenage girls and children, complaining
to me and Marais about the transformation. They mourned the disappearance of
the Beast—the same Beast who terrified
them so at the time when Madame
Leprince de Beaumont wrote the tale."

Oskar Fischinger.
**Motion Painting I**.
1947

In 1936 Oskar Fischinger accepted an invitation from Paramount to come to America and work in Hollywood. In Germany he had been a distinguished inventor, theorist, and maker of abstract and industrial short films. Once in the United States, however, he soon found himself at odds with the factorylike methods of the major studios, and sought expression in the creation of independently financed experimental films. His greatest achievement in this field, and his last completed project, is *Motion Painting I*. A film of extraordinary beauty and rhythmic power, it is an abstract work created by painting with oils on Plexiglas. Set to an excerpt from J. S. Bach's Brandenburg Concerto no. 3, it comprises an exuberant series of intricate transformations—one every twenty-fourth of a second—that explore the dynamic relationship between sound and image, and the film's unique combination of visual and aural tonalities never ceases to amaze and charm. *Motion Painting I* is a testament to Fischinger's passion for experimentation and invention.

Jules Dassin.
**Brute Force**. 1947.
*Burt Lancaster*

David Lean.
**Great Expectations**.
1946. *Jean Simmons,
Valerie Hobson,
Anthony Wager*

Vittorio De Sica.
**Ladri di biciclette
(The Bicycle
Thief).** 1948.
*Lamberto Maggiorani,
Enzo Staiola*

H. C. Potter.
**Mr. Blandings
Builds His Dream
House.** 1948.
*Myrna Loy,
Cary Grant*

John Huston.
**Key Largo**. 1948.
*Lauren Bacall,*
*Humphrey Bogart*

Preston Sturges.
**Unfaithfully Yours**.
1948. *Linda Darnell,*
*Rex Harrison*

When producer Dore Schary hired Joseph Losey to direct *The Boy with Green Hair*, Losey was almost forty years old and had already enjoyed a long and varied career in theater and radio. In addition to writing book and theater reviews for various New York City newspapers and magazines, he spent the 1930s and 1940s as a stage manager and director, attended film classes in Moscow taught by Sergei Eisenstein, helped create the theater style "The Living Newspaper" for the New York stage, supervised dozens of documentary short subjects for the Rockefeller Foundation, and, immediately preceding his contract with Schary, directed Charles Laughton on stage in Bertolt Brecht's *Galileo*. *The Boy with Green Hair*, of a piece with this body of politically and socially aware work, is both a parable about war and its effects on children worldwide and a plea for tolerance of the foreign or strange. Peter (Dean Stockwell), a war orphan who is moved from one foster home to another until he settles in with Gramps (played with affecting understatement by veteran Pat O'Brien), wakes up one day with green hair. Despite his best efforts to embrace the transformation, he is persecuted by the townspeople until he agrees to have his head shaved clean. When the town gathers around to see Peter's offending hair cut away, the sadness and humiliation of the moment are palpable, anchoring this otherwise light allegorical film to the harsh realities of life.

Georges Rouquier.
**Farrebique**. 1948

Robert J. Flaherty.
**Louisiana Story**.
1948. *Joseph
Boudreau*

*Opposite:*
Norman McLaren.
**Begone Dull
Care**. 1949

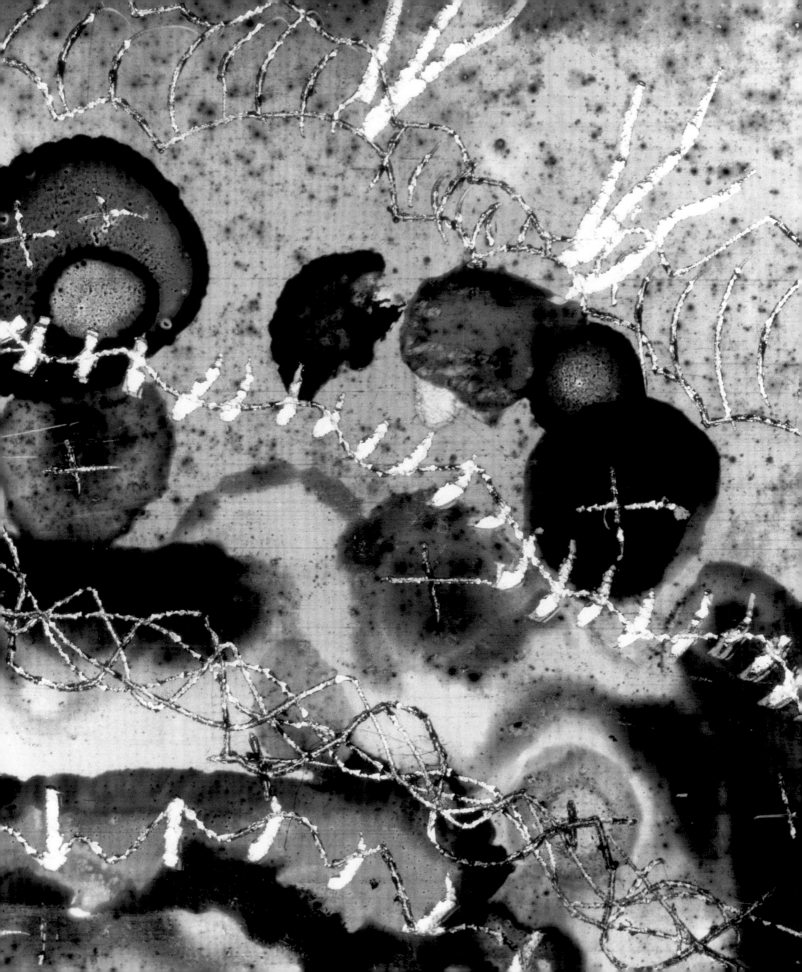

Luis Buñuel.
**Los olvidados**.
1950. *Alfonso Mejía,
Roberto Cobo*

Joseph L.
Mankiewicz.
**All About Eve**.
1950. *Gary Merrill
(hidden), Anne Baxter,
Celeste Holm, George
Sanders, Marilyn
Monroe, Bette Davis,
Hugh Marlowe*

George Cukor.
**Born Yesterday**.
1951. *Judy Holliday,
Broderick Crawford,
William Holden*

Roberto Rossellini.
**Francesco,
giullare di Dio**.
1950. *Nazario
Gerardi, Arabella
Lemaitre*

*Opposite:*
Vittorio De Sica.
**Miracolo a Milano
(Miracle in
Milan).** 1950.
*Brunella Bovo,
Francesco Golisano*

Federico Fellini.
**Lo sceicco bianco
(The White
Sheik).** 1952.
*Alberto Sordi
(on swing)*

Adapted for the screen by Cesare Zavattini
and Vittorio De Sica from the former's
novel *Totò il buono* (1940), *Miracolo a
Milano* is a powerful work of social
protest in the guise of allegorical fantasy.
When young Totò's elderly guardian,
Lolotta, dies, he takes up with the inhabitants of a shantytown on the outskirts of
Milan. The residents are battling a rich
man who wants to take their land in order
to dig for oil. Lolotta's spirit sends Totò
and the slum dwellers help in the form of
a magic dove, and after several complica-
tions, the dove leads them through the
sky to a better world. Famous for such
Neorealist landmarks as *Ladri di biciclette*
(*The Bicycle Thief*, 1949) and *Umberto D*
(1952), director De Sica and screenwriter
Zavattini here depart from their usually
tough yet sentimental style of filmmaking, offering instead a fanciful solution to
Italy's postwar woes. The final flight by
the shantytown residents over Milan on
broomsticks perfectly captures the duo's
frank admission that only an event of
miraculous proportions could solve the
problems of Italy's unfortunates.

Howard Hawks.
**The Big Sky**.
1952. *Arthur
Hunnicut, Dewey
Martin, Kirk
Douglas*

*Left:*
George Cukor.
**The Marrying
Kind**. 1952. *Aldo
Ray, Judy Holliday*

*Below, left:*
Roberto Rossellini.
**Viaggio in Italia**.
1954. *Ingrid Bergman*

*Below:*
Vincent J. Donehue.
**The Trip to
Bountiful**. 1953.
*Lillian Gish,
Eva Marie Saint*

217

1950s

Yasujiro Ozu.
**Tokyo monogatari
(Tokyo Story)**.
1953. *Chiyeko
Higashiyama,
Setsuko Hara*

Vincente Minnelli.
**The Band Wagon**.
1953. *Cyd Charisse,
Fred Astaire*

Ray Ashley, Morris Engel, and Ruth Orkin. **Little Fugitive**. 1953. *Richie Andrusco*

Seven-year-old Joey lives with his mother and older brother, Lennie, in Brooklyn. When Joey is left in Lennie's care, the older boy tricks Joey into believing that he has murdered him, and the youngster runs away to Coney Island. Once there, he has a day filled with adventures. Using a small, portable 35mm camera of his own devising, codirector Morris Engel unobtrusively followed the boy around the Brooklyn boardwalk and environs, giving him free rein to encounter and react spontaneously to the world into which he had been placed. Whether filming young actor Richie Andrusco on the parachute jump, on a horse ride, in a batting cage, or scrounging under the boardwalk for empty soda bottles to redeem for badly needed cash, Engel and Orkin never lose sight of the boy's perspective, making this a deeply affecting look at life from a child's point of view. In its feeling of improvisation, as well as in its commitment to a direct and unfiltered recording of real life as it occurs, this unprecedented film looks forward both to the documentary movement of the next decade, known as cinema verité, and to the French Nouvelle Vague. As François Truffaut later claimed, "Our New Wave would never have come into being if it hadn't been for the young Morris Engel…with his fine *Little Fugitive*."

Federico Fellini.
**I vitelloni**. 1953.
*Alberto Sordi (far right)*

George Cukor.
**It Should Happen to You**. 1954.
*Judy Holliday, Jack Lemmon*

Herbert J. Biberman.
**Salt of the Earth**.
1954. *Rosaura Revueltas, Will Geer (as sheriff)*

# The Joseph Cornell Collection

Joseph Cornell was an American original. Born in 1903 in Nyack, a busy Hudson River town just north of New York City, as a teenager he moved with his family to a house on Utopia Parkway in Flushing, at that time a near-rural neighborhood in the borough of Queens, and lived there until his death in 1972. Although famously shy, Cornell was anything but reclusive. He worked for many years as a designer in the textiles industry and in his spare time created sculptural and cinematic assemblages of exceptional delicacy and beauty. Like the box constructions for which he is best known, his films are sui generis, influenced by the Dada and Surrealist movements of the early twentieth century, certainly, but also containing a distinctive, personal quality: a deep nostalgia for a quasi-mythical Victorian past, as well as for the silent films of his youth and the screen divas to whom he was passionately devoted.

Cornell was an obsessive collector of the detritus of popular and material culture, using these found objects in both his sculptures and his films. For the latter, he would buy 16mm prints of what were, for the time, obscure or utterly forgotten films, then cut them up and edit them together into dreamscapes of his subconscious; *Rose Hobart* (c. 1936), made up of pieces of the Hollywood film *East of Borneo* (George Melford, 1931) and named for its leading lady, is one such work. Together with filmmakers such as Stan Brakhage, Rudy Burkhardt, and Larry Jordan, he would travel the city's streets in search of fleeting moments that could be captured on film and then carefully assemble them into flights of film fancy; *Nymphlight* (1957) and *The Aviary* (1955) are examples of this process. Cornell identified with no partic-

Joseph Cornell.
**Rose Hobart**.
c. 1936

ular school of filmmaking, nor did he propound any theories of film; rather, he immersed himself in his raw materials and emerged with works of art that contained the universe in miniature.

In 1995 The Joseph and Robert Cornell Memorial Foundation donated to The Museum of Modern Art all of the film materials that were in the artist's possession at the time of his death. The collection contains negatives and prints of Cornell's own finished films, as well as numerous short and feature films that he purchased over a lifetime of collecting. Cornell was particularly intrigued by early French cinema, and the collection contains 16mm copies of films by such artists as Georges Méliès, Émile Cohl, Ferdinand Zecca, Lucien Nonguet, and the Lumière brothers. For this reason, the Joseph Cornell Collection is not just an important record of the artist's own output but also of his working methods and his personal passions.

Joseph Cornell.
**By Night with
Torch and Spear**.
n.d. Preserved by
Anthology Film
Archives, 1979

Joseph Cornell and
Rudy Burckhardt.
**Nymphlight**. 1957

Joseph Cornell.
**Bookstalls**. Late
1930s. Preserved by
Anthology Film
Archives, 1978

Joseph Cornell.
**The Midnight
Party**. c. 1938.
Effects added by
Larry Jordan,
1965–68

Joseph Cornell and
Rudy Burckhardt.
**The Aviary**.
1954–55

Elia Kazan.
**On the Waterfront**.
1954. *Marlon Brando,*
*Eva Marie Saint*

Charles Laughton.
**The Night of the**
**Hunter**. 1955.
*Shelley Winters,*
*Robert Mitchum*

Carl Theodor
Dreyer. **Ordet**. 1955.
*Cay Kristiansen,*
*Birgitte Federspiel,*
*Henrik Malberg*

John Ford.
**The Searchers**.
1956. *Harry Carey, Jr.,*
*Jeffrey Hunter,*
*John Wayne*

Satyajit Ray.
**Pather Panchali**.
1955. *Subir Banerjee*

In *Pather Panchali*, the tale of a poor family living in its ancestral Bengali village, Satyajit Ray employed unknown actors and shot the film on location. His use of Neorealist techniques challenged the melodramatic song-and-dance form then characteristic of Indian cinema. Over the course of this film and its two sequels, *Aparajito* (1957) and *The World of Apu* (1959), viewers witness the world through the eyes of the young Apu, whose developing consciousness parallels the changing face of a newly independent India.

A filmmaker who could capture the essential themes of his culture while also evoking universal truths and values, Ray is recognized worldwide as a great poetic realist. In the early 1950s, he was working as a graphic artist when he decided to make a film from a book he was illustrating, the popular serial novel *Pather Panchali*. Ray had great difficulty financing his film throughout its production, and much of the work was done by amateurs. Although Ray was dissatisfied with its technical shortcomings, *Pather Panchali*, which had its theatrical debut in a special screening at The Museum of Modern Art in 1955, is widely admired for its casual and direct style.

Francis Thompson.
**N.Y., N.Y.** 1957

Alfred Hitchcock.
**Vertigo**. 1958.
*James Stewart,
Kim Novak*

Jerome Hill.
**Albert
Schweitzer**. 1957

Alain Resnais.
**Hiroshima, mon
amour**. 1959.
*Eiji Okada,
Emmanuèle Riva*

While making a film in Japan, a French actress has an affair with a Japanese architect. As their relationship unfolds, the story of her life in occupied France as the lover of a German soldier, as well as her subsequent condemnation as a collaborator, is interwoven with his horrific experiences as a survivor of the atomic bombing of Hiroshima. Both are married, to all appearances happily so, yet they are drawn to each other in subtle, unspoken ways. Director Alain Resnais's images and screenwriter Marguerite Duras's words present the story in a series of searing flashbacks, brief vignettes that sometimes leave the viewer unsure whether the date is 1959 or 1945. This jumbling of time produces a sense of timelessness, of course, but it also impresses one with the contingent nature of reality and, most importantly, truth. The two lovers, knowing their relationship is fleeting, challenge and soothe each other in equal measure, so as to savor every moment they have together. This lack of a traditional narrative structure, combined with the understated performances by Emmanuèle Riva and Eiji Okada in the lead roles, disturbed audiences in 1959, leaving many with the idea that Resnais, who had only recently turned to fiction features after a distinguished career directing documentaries (among them, 1955's *Nuit et brouillard*), was either incompetent or hopelessly pretentious. Time has proved otherwise, and Resnais's subsequent body of work has more than rewarded the close attention of sympathetic viewers.

Willard Van Dyke
and Shirley Clarke.
**Skyscraper**. 1959

# 1960s

Federico Fellini.
**La dolce vita**.
1960. *Marcello
Mastroianni (far
right)*

Ben Maddow,
Sidney Meyers, and
Joseph Strick.
**The Savage Eye**.
1960

John Cassavetes.
**Shadows**. 1961.
*Lelia Goldoni,
Anthony Ray*

Satyajit Ray.
**Teen kanya (Two
Daughters)**. 1961.
*Chandana Banerjee,
Anil Chatterjee*

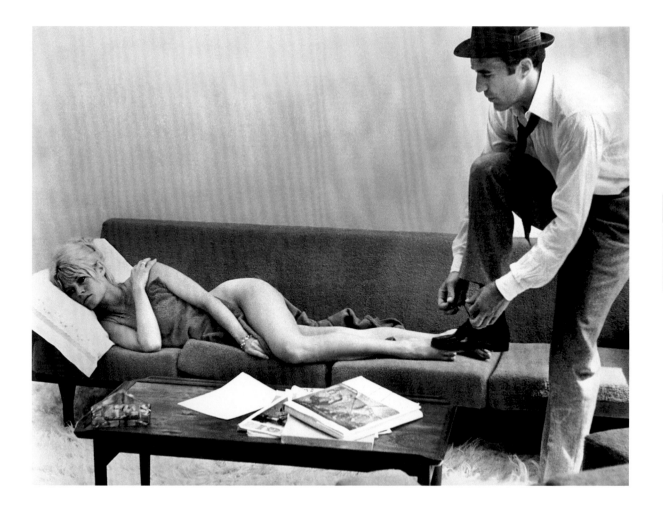

Jean-Luc Godard.
**Le Mépris (Contempt)**. 1963.
*Brigitte Bardot,
Michel Piccoli*

Elia Kazan.
**America America**.
1963. *Elena Karam,
Stathis Giallelis*

Stan VanDerBeek.
**Breathdeath**. 1964

Michelangelo
Antonioni.
**Il deserto rosso
(Red Desert)**.
1964. *Monica Vitti*

*Opposite:*
Federico Fellini.
**8½**. 1963.
*Marcello Mastroianni*

Sidney Lumet.
**Fail-Safe**. 1964.
*Edward Binns*

The nuclear politics of the Cold War inspired numerous films dealing with the life-and-death, cat-and-mouse maneuverings of the two great world powers, but none was so genuinely chilling as *Fail-Safe*. Based on the best-selling novel by Eugene Burdick and Harvey Wheeler, Sidney Lumet's film tells the story of a squadron of American jet bombers on a routine reconnaissance flight that, due to a computer malfunction, receives an irrevocable order to drop its nuclear payload on Moscow. Every effort by U.S. commanders, including a verbal order to the pilot from the president himself, as well as air and ground attacks by both American and Soviet forces, fails to stop the planes. The final outcome, in which both the Soviet capital and New York City are obliterated, is the fulfillment of humanity's worst nightmare. The film, an utterly dark cautionary tale about the necessity of developing procedures to forestall this sort of outcome, demonstrates how, despite their best intentions, politicians, professional soldiers, and academic experts are as helpless as anyone else in the face of their "foolproof" weapons systems.

Federico Fellini.
**Giulietta degli spiriti (Juliet of the Spirits)**. 1965.
*Lou Gilbert, Sandra Milo*

Jean-Luc Godard.
**Alphaville, une étrange aventure de Lemmy Caution**. 1965.
*Anna Karina, Eddie Constantine*

# The Andy Warhol Collection

Andy Warhol bought his first motion picture camera, a silent 16mm Bolex, in 1963. Almost immediately, he began making films featuring members of his artistic circle—friends, fellow artists, dealers, musicians, hangers-on, and random visitors to the Factory, that beehive of activity that served as the crossroads of the contemporary New York art scene. At first, the duration of the films was determined by the size of the film roll that the Bolex could accommodate—one hundred feet for *Sleep* (1964) and *Haircut* (1963)—but over time, Warhol combined rolls to make longer films, such as *Kiss* (1964). All were silent, and Warhol maximized the running time of each by shooting the films at twenty-four frames per second but projecting them at sixteen. One silent, minimalist epic after another rolled out of the Factory in 1963 and 1964.

Near the end of 1964, a second camera was added to his arsenal: a 16mm Auricon, which used synchronized sound and could accommodate larger (1,200-foot) rolls of film. By using this camera to shoot his feature-length films, Warhol was able to free up the Bolex to continue making his smaller films, especially the screen tests, a series of films that he had begun in 1963 and which he would continue to shoot through 1966. This series eventually came to number 472 films, each one a unique portrait of a sitter usually photographed from the shoulders up, against a neutral background, and instructed to move as little as possible. This last directive wasn't always easy to follow, as each screen test was one continuous take lasting the entire length of the one-hundred-foot roll of film. Some subjects remained perfectly still, others fidgeted uncomfortably, and still others just gave up and left the frame. Each *Screen Test*, however, regardless of its outcome, is a compelling still portrait in moving pictures; taken as a whole, they may very well constitute Warhol's greatest achievement as a filmmaker.

The preservation of Warhol's films began in the late 1980s, as a joint project between The Museum of Modern Art, the Andy Warhol Foundation for the Visual Arts, and the Whitney Museum of American Art. The Museum of Modern Art catalogued, stored, and preserved Warhol's films, while the Whitney undertook the scholarly research on the films and produced a catalogue raisonné. The Foundation underwrote the entire project (and in 1997 donated all of Warhol's original film elements to the Museum). This unprecedented collaboration has resulted in the conservation and circulation of these films for the first time in over thirty years, and has sparked a long-overdue reassessment of Warhol's place in the history of cinema.

Andy Warhol.
**Kiss**. 1964.
*Jane Holzer;
Gerard Malanga*

244

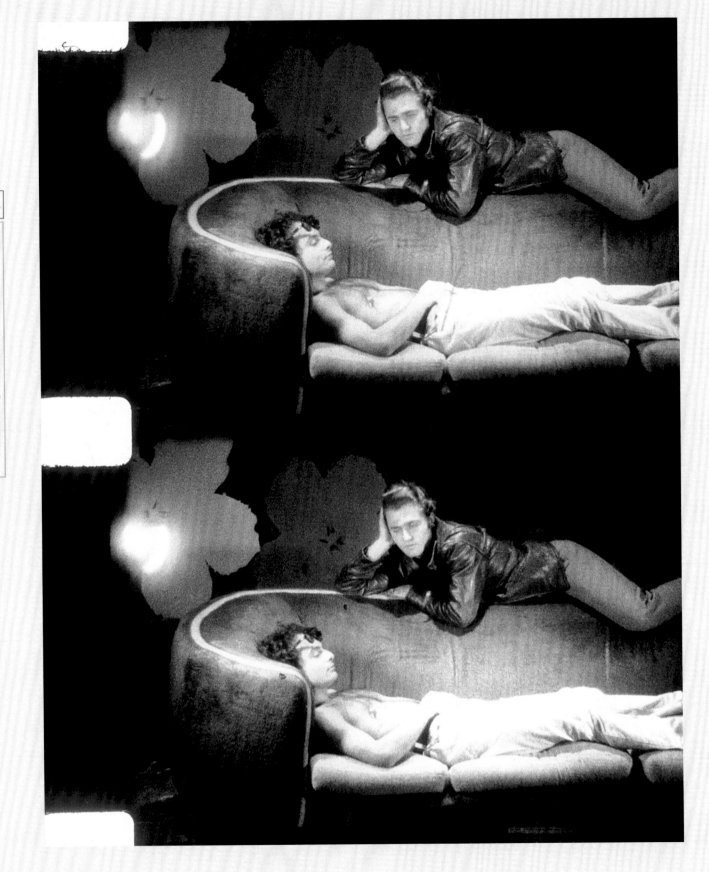

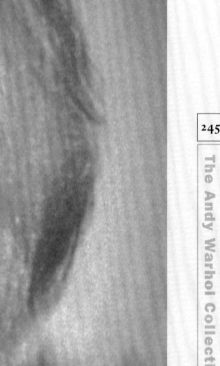

Andy Warhol.
**Screen Test: Jane
Holzer.** 1964

*Opposite:*
Andy Warhol.
**Couch.** 1964.
*Piero Heliczer,
Gerard Malanga*

Among the works contained in the Museum's Andy Warhol Collection are approximately 472 portrait films made by the artist between 1963 and 1966, the period in which he achieved his revolutionary vision of celebrity. Using a stationary camera, Warhol manipulated light and shadow in increasingly inventive ways to capture the appearance, style, personality, and mood of both famous and lesser-known visitors to his studio, the Factory. For each silent black-and-white film portrait, subjects—including "Baby Jane" Holzer (who appears in seven separate screen tests and is seen here chewing gum), Cass Elliott, Dennis Hopper, Gerard Malanga, Beverly Grant, Edie Sedgwick,

Susan Sontag, and Salvador Dalí, among others—were seated, instructed not to move, and filmed straight-on (most often in close-up). Although each film was shot at standard sound speed (twenty-four frames per second), Warhol specified that the prints be projected at a slower speed of sixteen frames per second, a rate normally used in the projection of silent films. The result is an unusual fluidity of pace—a rhythm gently at odds with the starkness of the lighting and the boldness of the close-ups. These arresting and influential works are innovative both as film and photograph, reinventing traditional portraiture through deceptively simple means.

Warhol at the
camera, shooting a
screen test, Gerard
Malanga at left,
c. 1965.

Andy Warhol.
**Harlot**. 1965.
*Gerard Malanga,
Philip Fagan,
Mario Montez,
Carol Koshinskie*

*Opposite:*
Andy Warhol.
**The Chelsea
Girls**. 1966. *Ondine*

Stanley Kubrick.
**2001: A Space
Odyssey**. 1968.
*Gary Lockwood,
Keir Dullea*

*Opposite, bottom:*
Bruce Nauman.
**Lip Sync**. 1969

In Bruce Nauman's *Lip Sync*, a video camera is turned upside down and held in a tight close-up on the filmmaker's face as he speaks the words of the title. The words, which at first emerge in a low murmur, quickly grow louder and more distinct, overwhelming the sound track and creating a rhythmic beat. The sound and image fall in and out of synchronization as the viewer tries vainly to connect the movement of Nauman's lips with his voice. This struggle intensifies as the work progresses, keeping the viewer in a state of nervous tension. Ultimately, the artist and the viewer become participants in a dance, both physical and intellectual, that is never reconciled, and in which moving images and sounds spiral around each other until the piece's conceptual framework appears ready to implode—yet never does.

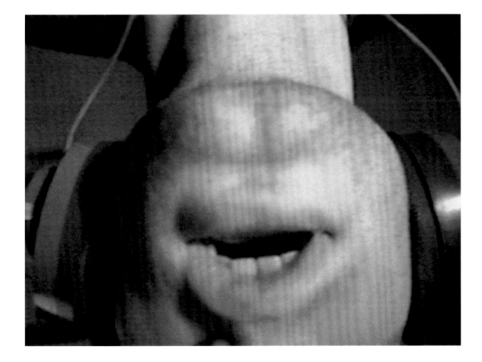

# 1970s

Ernie Gehr.
**Serene Velocity.**
1970

Dan Van Vliet.
**Lick My Decals
Off, Baby.** 1970

James Herbert.
**Porch Glider.**
1970

Peter Fonda.
**The Hired Hand**.
1971

Harry Hurwitz.
**The Projectionist**.
1970. *Jara Kohout,
Chuck McCann,
Ina Balin*

John Baldessari.
**I Am Making Art**.
1971

Paul Kos.
**Warlock(ing)**. 1971

*Right:*
Melvin Van Peebles.
**Sweet Sweetback's
Baadasssss Song**.
1971. *Melvin Van
Peebles*

It would be difficult to underestimate Melvin Van Peebles's achievement in producing, directing, writing, scoring, and starring in this film, not to mention financing it with the salary he had earned while directing *Watermelon Man* (1970). Not since Oscar Micheaux had an African American filmmaker taken such complete control of the creative process, turning out a work so deeply connected to his own personal and cultural reality that he was not surprised when the white critical establishment professed bewilderment upon its release in 1971. Filled with enough sex, rage, and violence to earn it an X rating, the success of *Sweet Sweetback's Baadasssss Song* depends less on its story of a superstud running from the police than it does on its disinterest in referencing white culture and its radically new understanding of how style and substance inform each other.

Jerome Hill.
**Film Portrait**.
1972

Born and raised in St. Paul, Minnesota, Jerome Hill, heir to a railroad fortune, was a writer, painter, and composer who is best known today for his film diaries and award-winning documentaries (*Albert Schweitzer*, 1957, and *Grandma Moses*, 1950). Completed shortly before Hill's death in 1972, *Film Portrait* is the summation of his life's work in film, a vivid collage of home movies, earlier short films, and found footage. The film spans Hill's entire biography, from his privileged and happy childhood in a wealthy Midwestern family through his restless adult years spent in quest of personal and artistic fulfillment. Heavily influenced both thematically and formally by cinema pioneers like Georges Méliès and the Lumière brothers, he also worked as a film artist at the same time that American avant-garde cinema came to maturity. As a result, *Film Portrait* is also the record of a movement—a film about Film. Happily, *Film Portrait*, which premiered at The Museum of Modern Art—and other films in the Museum's Jerome Hill Collection—are currently being restored with the generous support of the Jerome Foundation.

Ed Emshwiller.
**Scape-Mates**.
1972

Keith Sonnier.
**TV In TV Out.**
1972

Gilbert and George.
**Gordon Makes Us
Drunk.** 1972

Joan Jonas.
**Vertical Roll**. 1972

Nam June Paik.
**Global Groove**.
1973. *Charlotte
Moorman*

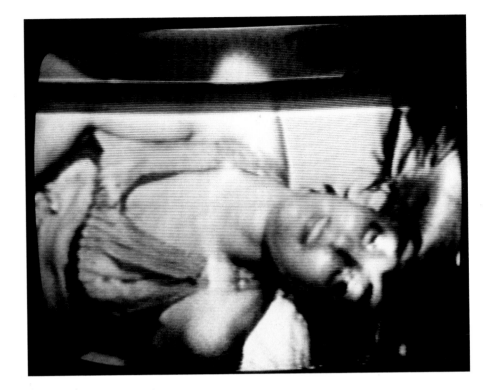

Luis Buñuel.
**Le Charme discret
de la bourgeoisie
(The Discreet
Charm of the
Bourgeoisie).** 1972

Vito Acconci.
**Theme Song**.
1973

Bill Gunn.
**Ganja and Hess**.
1973. *Duane Jones,*
*Sam Waymon*

Peter Campus.
**Three Transitions**.
1973

In *Three Transitions*, Peter Campus presents a trio of introspective self-portraits. He begins with an image created by two cameras facing opposite sides of a paper wall and filming simultaneously. With his back to one camera, Campus cuts through the paper. In the double image, it appears as if he were cutting through his own back, a suggestion both disconcerting and tongue-in-cheek. Campus then uses the "chroma key" effect of superimposing one video image onto a similarly colored area of another image. He applies blue paint to his face, revealing in this process yet another image of himself, which he then superimposes onto a piece of blue paper and sets on fire. As *Three Transitions* moves between deadpan humor and seeming self-destruction, Campus explores the limits of perception as a measure of reality.

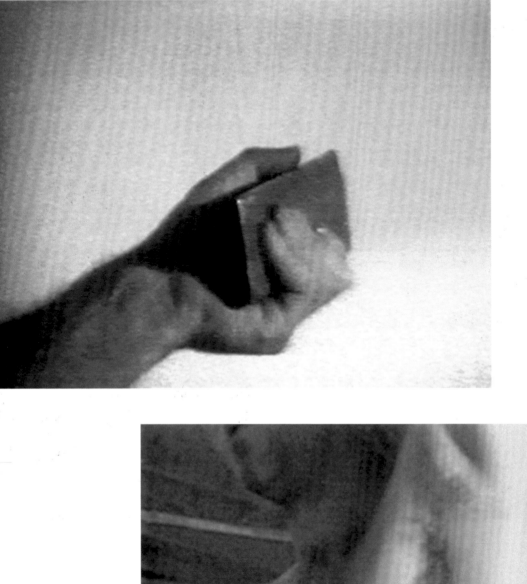

Richard Serra.
**Surprise Attack**.
1973

William Wegman.
**Reel No. 3**. 1973

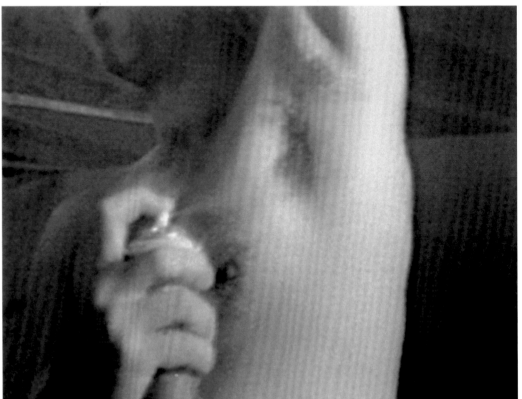

Stan Brakhage.
**The Text of
Light**. 1974

Beginning in the 1950s, Stan Brakhage,
America's most prolific and preeminent
avant-garde filmmaker, pursued what he
called the "art of vision," using processes
of layering, repetition of elements,
accumulations of details, juxtapositions
of unrelated images, and nonnarrative
sequences in his experimental films. Many
of his works draw from autobiographical
experiences, with images of family members and events from his daily life, but
others are more limited in scope, inspired
by the properties of filmmaking itself. By
the 1970s, Brakhage had intensified his
exploration of cinema's formal properties,
and he became intrigued by two of film's
basic means of expression: the apparent
motility of light and the resultant texture
of the transient image. *The Text of Light*,
a spare study of light moving through a
glass ashtray, is the purest result of this
investigation.

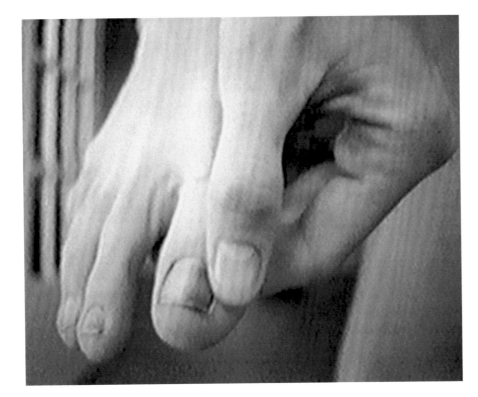

Lisa Steele.
**Birthday Suit—
With Scars and
Defects**. 1974

Hermine Freed.
**Art Herstory**.
1974

Martin Scorsese.
**ItalianAmerican**.
1974. *Martin
Scorsese, Charles
Scorsese, Catherine
Scorsese*

After having made four well-received feature films, among them *Mean Streets*
(1973), an uncompromising story of petty
criminals in New York City's Little Italy,
and *Alice Doesn't Live Here Anymore*
(1974), the tale of a single mother's journey to self-sufficiency, Martin Scorsese
stepped back briefly from his commercial
film career to make a small, deeply personal documentary. Shot on 16mm film in
the Manhattan apartment where he grew
up, *ItalianAmerican* is the record of a conversation between Scorsese and his parents, Charles and Catherine. In three-
quarters of an hour, the three manage to
cover a great deal of ground, most notably
the parents' experiences growing up in the
rough-and-tumble New York tenements
during the early years of the twentieth
century. Scorsese's presentation of his par-

ents is highly particularized and subtly
nuanced, yet he also manages to make
their words speak for the larger immigrant experience. When the setting shifts
from the living room to the dining room
and everyone sits down to dinner, the
mood becomes looser and more animated,
with Scorsese and his mother moving into
the kitchen for a quick lesson on how to
make tomato sauce—or "gravy," as
Catherine (and an entire generation of
Italian Americans) would call it. Throughout, the affection that the three Scorseses
have for each other is palpable, as is the
respect with which the son presents his
parents' story. At the end, Catherine's
recipe for her tomato sauce scrolls by on-
screen, making *ItalianAmerican* not only a
historical record, but also a family legacy.

Martha Rosler.
**Semiotics of the
Kitchen**. 1975

Francis Ford Coppola.
**The Conversation**.
1974. *Gene Hackman*

Steven Spielberg.
**Jaws**. 1975. *Robert
Shaw, Roy Scheider,
Richard Dreyfuss*

Ant Farm.
**Media Burn**. 1975

Shigeko Kubota.
**My Father**.
1973–75

Charles Atlas and
Merce Cunningham.
**Blue Studio**. 1976

Produced at WNET, New York City's public television station, *Blue Studio* is a new form of moving image art called "videodance," developed by Merce Cunningham specifically for the two-dimensional video monitor and realized in 1976 by Cunningham's filmmaker-in-residence at the time, Charles Atlas. The title of the piece comes from the technique known as "chroma key," in which any kind of background imagery imaginable can be superimposed upon the blue area of a video screen. Through this technology, as well as other video devices, Cunningham is transported into a varied series of outdoor landscapes while never actually leaving the confines of his studio. A disjunctive sound collage using the voices of John Cage and Jasper Johns completes the illusion. In its creation of an impossible yet magically fluid dance space, *Blue Studio* recalls Maya Deren's *Study in Choreography for Camera* (1945).

*Opposite:*
Martin Scorsese.
**Taxi Driver**. 1976.
*Jodie Foster*

Bill Viola.
**The Space
Between the
Teeth**. 1976

Peter Campus.
**num**. 1976

Susan Raymond
and Alan Raymond.
**Police Tapes**.
1976

Linda Montano.
**Mitchell's Death**.
1977

Bill Viola.
**Chott el-Djerid
(A Portrait in
Light and Heat).**
1979

*Chott el-Djerid (A Portrait in Light and Heat)*
captures the optical and acoustic distor-
tions of nature as if by magic. Focused on
landscape, the work dwells briefly on the
snowy plains of Midwestern America and
Saskatchewan, then abruptly switches to
the arid Tunisian desert. Bill Viola investi-
gates the world of illusion and how it is
made. Painstakingly uncovering the distinctive character of a place, he probes its
power and energy, drawing upon the asso-
ciations it evokes and searching instinc-
tively for its archetypal symbols.

To shoot *Chott el-Djerid*, Viola used a
video camera set on a tripod and meticu-
lously framed each subject from a fixed
vantage point. He only began filming
when he considered the atmospheric conditions to be ideal; at times he waited for
up to several days to start work. The
sound track is filled with ambient natural
sounds that temper the video's other-
worldly feel, but the work's pace compels
viewers to assume a mindset of dreamlike,
suspended animation.

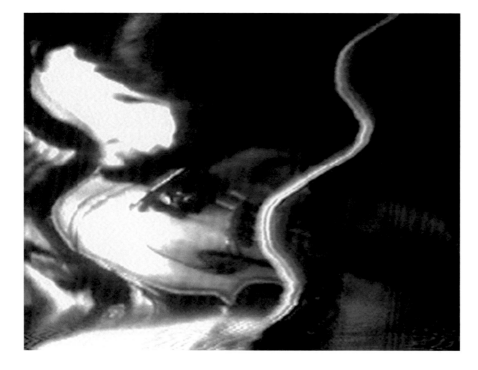

John Sturgeon.
**2 Aspects**. 1976

Steina Vasulka.
**Violin Power**.
1970–78

Rainer Werner
Fassbinder.
**Die Ehe der
Maria Braun (The
Marriage of Maria
Braun).** 1978.
*Hanna Schygulla,
George Byrd*

General Idea.
**Test Tube.** 1979

# 1980s

*Opposite:*
Martin Scorsese.
**Raging Bull**. 1980.
*Robert De Niro*

*Right:*
Louis Malle.
**Atlantic City**.
1980. *Burt Lancaster*

Tony Oursler.
**The Loner**. 1980

Hector Babenco.
**Pixote**. 1980.
*Fernando Ramos da
Silva (left)*

Lino Brocka.
**Bona**. 1980.
*Phillip Salvador;
Nora Aunor*

Lino Brocka made more than fifty films in a career that lasted barely twenty years. Starting as a script supervisor, he made his directorial debut in 1970 with *Wanted: Perfect Mother*. After a short series of commercial studio releases, Brocka withdrew from filmmaking altogether, returning to the business in 1974 with his own short-lived production company, CineManila, which folded two years later. From 1976 until his death in 1991, Brocka juggled commercial and personal projects, gaining an international reputation as the finest Philippine director of his generation. *Bona*, released in 1980, is perhaps his best-regarded work. The title character is a young, starstruck schoolgirl (played by Nora Aunor) who falls in love with an aging actor (Phillip Salvador) and becomes his servant. She waits on him loyally in his

decrepit shack, receiving nothing for her labors but the privilege of being his slave. When the actor decides he has had enough of her and attempts to toss her aside, Bona retaliates in a wholly unexpected, utterly justified fit of violent rage. As with many of his other independently made films, *Bona* reveals Brocka's uncanny ability to join the personal and the political, to locate the overarching social statement in an intimate, deeply individualized gesture. He gave voice to an enormous swath of the Filipino population, one that had previously been given little attention by the nation's filmmakers, most of whom were more concerned with the dissemination of fantasy than with immersion into real life. In so doing, he became a hero to an entire generation of filmmakers in the Pacific Rim and beyond.

Robert Wilson.
**Deafman Glance**.
1981

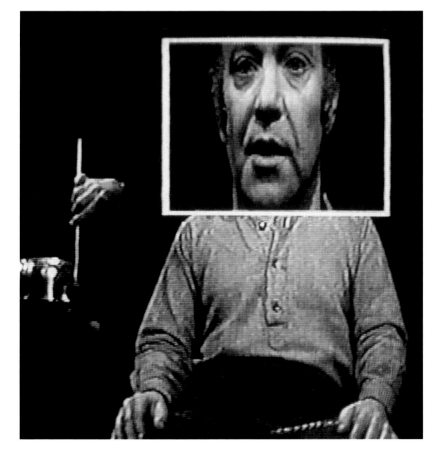

Paper Tiger
Television.
**Herb Schiller
Reads** *The New
York Times*. 1981

Shirley Clarke,
Joseph Chaiken,
and Sam Shepard.
**Tongues: Sav-
age/Love**. 1981

Krzysztof Kieślowski.
**Przypadek (Blind
Chance)**. 1982.
*Boguslaw Linda*

Cecilia Condit.
**Beneath the Skin**.
1981

Edin Vélez.
**Meta Mayan II**.
1981

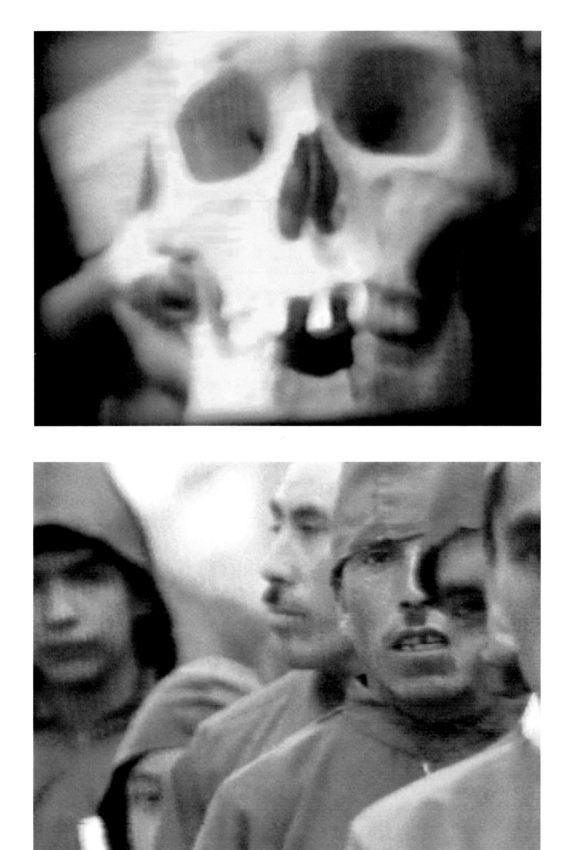

Bill Viola.
**Hatsu-Yume
(First Dream).**
1981

Barry Levinson.
**Diner**. 1982.
*Kevin Bacon, Mickey
Rourke, Daniel Stern,
Tim Daly*

Barry Levinson was already a successful
writer for television and movies (most
notably Mel Brooks's *High Anxiety*, 1977,
and *History of the World: Part 1*, 1988)
when he made his directorial debut with
*Diner*, a small film set in the Baltimore of
his youth. The story concerns the comings
and goings of a set of friends who are on
the brink of adulthood (marriage, careers,
etc.), yet who still find time to gather regularly at their favorite hangout to discuss
the really important things in life: sports,
music, girls, and food. The ensemble
cast—including Steve Guttenberg, Mickey
Rourke, Paul Reiser, Daniel Stern, Kevin
Bacon, Tim Daly, and Ellen Barkin—
does little that would be considered

dramatic or eventful in a more traditional
Hollywood film, but Levinson's attention
to character and period detail, as well as
his willingness to let those elements drive
his story, caught the imagination of audiences and critics alike. After the box office
success of *Diner*, Levinson quickly moved
on to projects with bigger stars and more
generous budgets (*The Natural*, 1984, *Good
Morning, Vietnam*, 1987, *Rain Man*, 1988).
Still, his heart remains in Baltimore, to
which he returned in three equally personal films (*Tin Men*, 1987, *Avalon*, 1990,
*Liberty Heights*, 1999). In 1999 Levinson
was instrumental in having all four of his
Baltimore films deposited in The Museum
of Modern Art's permanent collection.

Rainer Werner
Fassbinder.
**Die Sehnsucht
der Veronika Voss
(Veronika Voss)**.
1982. *Rosel Zech*

Paolo Taviani and
Vittorio Taviani.
**La notte di San
Lorenzo (The
Night of the
Shooting Stars)**.
1982. *Margarita
Lozano, Omero
Antonutti*

Marcel Odenbach.
**The Distance
between Myself
and My Losses**.
1983

Laurie Anderson.
**O Superman**. 1983

Dan Graham.
**Rock My
Religion**. 1984.
*Patti Smith*

Woody Allen.
**Broadway Danny
Rose**. 1984

Between the formal experimentation and psychological gamesmanship of *Zelig* (1983) and *The Purple Rose of Cairo* (1985), a bittersweet fantasy about the heart-breaking power of cinema, Woody Allen made *Broadway Danny Rose*, a straightforward and enormously funny valentine to those on the lowest rungs of the theatrical ladder. Allen plays the title character, a down-on-his-luck manager who represents such marginal "talent" as a balloon act, a blind xylophone player, skating penguins, and a water-glass musician. His one remotely successful client is Lou Canova, a singer he manages to book into the Waldorf-Astoria. When Canova insists that Danny go to New Jersey and pick up his mistress so that she can attend his

show, an unexpected odyssey through suburban Jersey and Manhattan ensues, leading to a contract on Danny's life. As with many of Allen's best films, the plot of *Broadway Danny Rose* is intricate and carefully laid out, but it is ultimately a mere hook on which to hang the many colorful characters and funny situations at which Woody Allen excels. There is no underlying message in this film, nor does it attempt to speak to any deeper human condition. *Broadway Danny Rose* is, simply, a comedy, a film designed to entertain and amuse. If it also manages to convey a sense of nostalgia for vaudeville's golden age, that is just a result of its director engaging in a bit of well-earned wistfulness.

Lizzie Borden.
**Born in Flames**.
1983

Mako Idemitsu.
**Hideo: It's Me,
Mama**. 1983

Beth B.
**The Dominatrix
Sleeps Tonight**.
1984

*Opposite:*
Shalom Gorewitz.
**Black Fire**. 1986

*Above:*
Jim Jarmusch.
**Stranger Than
Paradise**. 1984.
*Richard Edson,
Eszter Balint,
John Lurie*

Woody Allen.
**Zelig**. 1983

Joan Jonas.
**Double Lunar
Dogs**. 1984

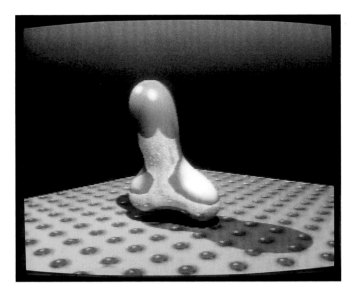

Masaki Fujihata.
**Maitreya**. 1984

David Byrne and
Stephen Johnson.
**Road to Nowhere**.
1985

1980s

Victor Masayesva. **Itam Hakim Hopiit (We Some-one, the Hopi People).** 1984

Leslie Thornton. **Peggy and Fred in Hell: The Pro-logue.** 1987–89

John Cassavetes.
**Love Streams**.
1984. *John Cassavetes,
Gena Rowlands*

Bill Sherwood.
**Parting Glances**.
1986. *Steve Buscemi*
*(right)*

Claude Lanzmann.
**Shoah**. 1985

la fin du voyage.

Oliver Stone.
**Platoon**. 1986

A Yale dropout who worked as a teacher in Saigon and later as a merchant seaman, Oliver Stone volunteered for infantry service during the Vietnam War. He was wounded in combat and earned a Bronze Star and a Purple Heart. After the war, he studied filmmaking at New York University, where one of his instructors was Martin Scorsese, and eventually made his mark as a screenwriter, most notably on *Midnight Express* (Alan Parker, 1978), for which he won the Oscar for best adapted screenplay. These were the raw materials that went into the making of *Platoon*, Stone's fourth feature film and the one that elevated him to the first rank of filmmakers. Working from his own script, he told the story of the common American foot soldier in Vietnam, avoiding the larger geopolitical issues of the conflict to focus on what life was like for the war's hundreds of thousands of young "grunts." The film seesaws between the tedium of camp life's daily routine and the shock of sudden, vicious combat, and no other filmmaker has ever captured so viscerally the stark terror of such warfare. *Platoon* is often melodramatic, even pretentious—occasional traits of this filmmaker—yet here Stone earns the right to such extremes. Whatever the film may lack in narrative polish or psychological subtlety, it conveys the emotional truth of combat itself. It is a generous and openhearted film, one in which Stone keeps faith with his former comrades-in-arms by explaining without ever excusing, by forgiving without forgetting.

Abigail Child.
**Mayhem**. 1987

George Kuchar.
**Creeping
Crimson**. 1987

*Opposite:*
Kathryn Bigelow.
**Near Dark**. 1987.
*Adrian Pasdar,
Jenny Wright*

Nathaniel Dorsky.
**Alaya.** 1987

Mary Lucier.
**Ohio to Giverny:
Memory of Light.**
1987

Woody Vasulka.
**The Art of
Memory**. 1987

The mythic and seemingly eternal land-scape of the American Southwest serves as the literal and suggestive backdrop for artist Woody Vasulka's *The Art of Memory*, in which images of war—the Russian Rev-olution, the Spanish Civil War, World War II, the nuclear stalemate of the Cold War—fragment and contort until meaning blurs and history attains the uncertainty of memory. A lone angel looks over this landscape and silently watches it pass by, mute witness to the tragedy that was the twentieth century. Vasulka has spent the better part of his artistic life interrogating the recorded image, teasing a multiplicity of meanings out of his subtle manipula-tions of film and video, and *The Art of Memory* may be viewed as a summing-up of that work, a collapsing of the porous distinctions between history and cultural memory.

*Above:*
Julie Zando.
**Let's Play
Prisoners**. 1988

*Above, right:*
Rhonda Abrams.
**The Lament of
the Sugar Bush
Man**. 1987

*Right:*
Eleanor Antin.
**From the
Archives of
Modern Art**. 1987

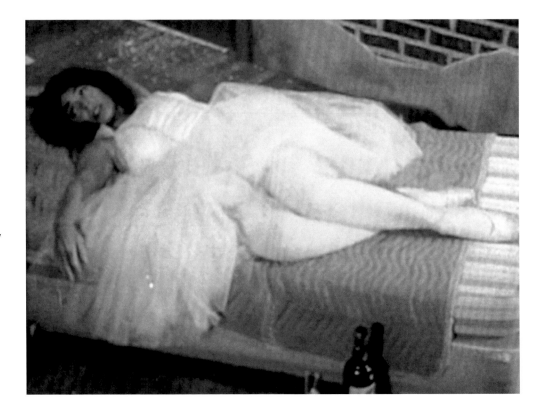

John Huston.
**The Dead**. 1987.
*Anjelica Huston
(far right)*

John Huston started in Hollywood as a screenwriter, working throughout the 1930s for such directors as William Wyler, Robert Florey, Anatole Litvak, William Dieterle, and Raoul Walsh until he got the chance to direct his own script for *The Maltese Falcon* (1941). In a directorial career that went on to span five decades and thirty-seven feature films, Huston made a specialty of literary adaptation, basing all but ten of his films on the work of authors as diverse as Herman Melville, Flannery O'Connor, Rudyard Kipling, Tennessee Williams, Dashiell Hammett, and B. Traven. Ever ready to take on new challenges, he turned to perhaps the most difficult author of all, James Joyce, for what proved to be his last film, *The Dead*.

Both the story and the film are set in Dublin and recount the events of a single night in January of 1904, in which an annual post-holiday party, filled with friends, good cheer, and hospitality, is followed by a wife's private and devastating confession to her husband of a long-ago love affair with a young man now dead. Huston, himself near death, drew upon deep wells of emotional and physical strength to see *The Dead* through to its completion, creating in the process a serenely beautiful work that acknowledges the all-too-human frailties of its characters without in any way absolving them of their responsibilities toward each other, or the past.

Jean-Luc Godard.
**Puissance de la
parole**. 1988

Jean-Luc Godard, one of cinema's most
influential artists, has made significant
contributions to the field of video. He
began making films in the mid-1950s, and
since 1974 he has been working with
video technologies, employing techniques
such as deconstruction, reassemblage, and
collage to create a fresh aesthetic that is
both resonant and intriguing. Godard
overlaps music, sounds, and dialogue and
establishes visual rhythms through juxta-
posing slow takes and rapid cuts to create
what he calls *son image*, that is, sound and
image. In *Puissance de la parole*, explosive
sequences from nature abut those consist-
ing of passionate discussions by two cou-
ples. One pair argues in dialogue spoken
by the lovers in the novel *The Postman
Always Rings Twice*, by James Cain; the
other couple quotes a tale by Edgar Allan
Poe. Regardless of his chosen medium,
Godard has always expressed a wide range
of thematic interests—art, politics, history,
television, communication, anxiety, sex,
desire, music, and the history of the movies.

Gary Hill.
**Incidents of
Catastrophe**. 1988

Mona Hatoum.
**Measures of
Distance**. 1988

*Opposite:*
Marlon Riggs.
**Tongues Untied**.
1989

*Above:*
Oliver Stone.
**Born on the
Fourth of July**.
1989. *Tom Cruise*

Gary Hill.
**Site/Recite**
**(a prologue).** 1989

Peter Callas.
**Neo-Geo: An**
**American Purchase.**
1989

Peggy Ahwesh.
**Martina's
Playhouse.** 1989

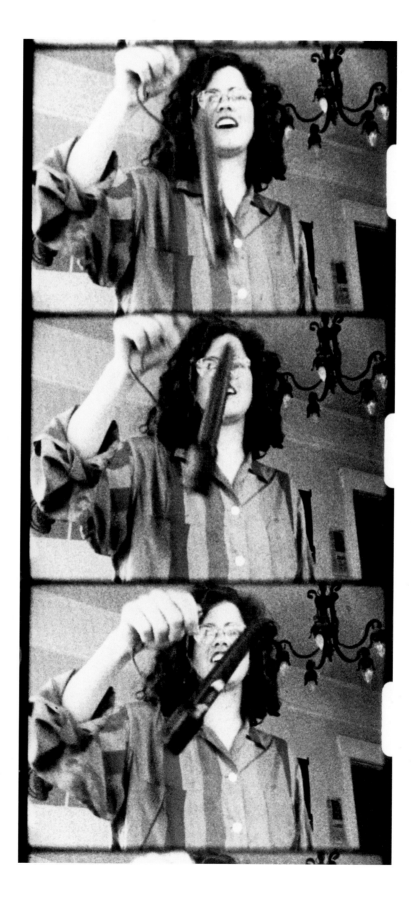

Martin Scorsese.
**The Last Temp-
tation of Christ**.
1989. *Willem Dafoe*

Spike Lee.
**Do the Right Thing**. 1989.
*Spike Lee (far right)*

Early in his career, Spike Lee was identified as America's leading black filmmaker for making movies in which personal and cultural politics are not only partisan, but aggressively so. He has worn this imposed mantle of seriousness nimbly, refusing to be pigeonholed into any particular genre or style. Unfortunately, by forcing him into the role of Black Filmmaker, critics and audiences have risked misunderstanding the reason for Spike Lee's success: he possesses a commanding mastery of the medium. This was made evident beyond doubt in his third theatrical feature, 1989's *Do the Right Thing*. Set during the course of a single, sweltering summer day in the Bedford-Stuyvesant neighborhood of Brooklyn, the film tracks the quickly growing tensions between an Italian American pizza-parlor owner and the local black residents. The specificity of the film's locale and characters allows writer/director Lee to explore themes and personalities that a more broadly drawn, simplistic piece of agitprop never could, and it is by locating the politics of the day's events in his individualized protagonists that Lee manages to pull off the film's cataclysmic finale with believability and conviction. Subsequent films would show Lee tackling equally explosive subject matter, and he would branch out with great success into a variety of genres, but few of his later productions, as accomplished as they are, would have the visceral, far-reaching impact of *Do the Right Thing*.

Martin Scorsese.
**Goodfellas**. 1990.
*Ray Liotta,*
*Lorraine Bracco*

*Opposite:*
Yvonne Rainer.
**Privilege**. 1990

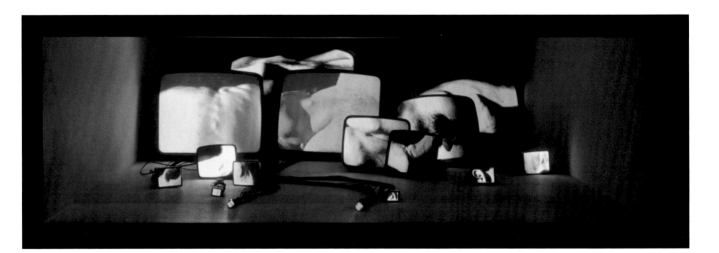

Gary Hill.
**Inasmuch As It Is
Always Already
Taking Place**.
1990

The components of the body displayed on the sixteen monitors in this video installation are without any apparent distinction. They belong, however, to the artist. The arrangement of images on the monitors, which are of various sizes and stripped of their casings, does not follow the organization of the human body. Representations of Gary Hill's ear and foot lie side by side; tucked modestly behind them is an image of his groin. Within this unassuming configuration, each screen invites meditation. For example, on one screen a thumb plays with the corner of a book page. By concentrating the viewer's attention on such a rudimentary activity, Hill causes the movement to take on the significance of a much larger event. Long, nervelike black wires attached to each monitor are bundled together like spinal cords, and a textured composition of ambient sound reinforces the living quality of the installation.

Antonio Muntadas.
**Between the
Frames**. 1983–91

Nick Gomez.
**Laws of Gravity**.
1991. *Peter Greene,
Edie Falco*

Antonio Muntadas.
**Between the
Frames**. 1983–91

Nick Gomez.
**Laws of Gravity**.
1991. *Peter Greene,
Edie Falco*

Julie Dash.
**Daughters of the
Dust**. 1991. *Alva
Rogers, Barbara O.
Jones, Cora Lee Day*

Shelly Silver.
**The Houses That
Are Left**. 1991

*Oppposite:*
Chris Marker.
**Le Tombeau d'Alexandre (The Last Bolshevik)**.
1992

*Right:*
Ernie Gehr.
**Side/Walk/Shuttle**.
1991

Critic J. Hoberman has described Ernie Gehr as "cinema's virtuoso minimalist," and *Side/Walk/Shuttle* is compelling evidence of this claim. As Gehr recalls, "The initial inspiration for the film was an outdoor glass elevator and the visual, spatial, and gravitational possibilities it presented me with. The work was also informed by an interest in panoramas, the urban landscape, as well as the topography of San Francisco. Finally, the shape and character of the work was tempered by reflections upon a lifetime of displacement, moving from place to place and haunted by recurring memories of other places I once passed through." The film consists of twenty-five moving shots, most less than ninety seconds in length and all taken from within the glass elevator of San Francisco's Fairmont Hotel. The city swoops and tilts before our eyes, making the viewer question the very laws of gravity. Indeed, the sense of wonder Gehr creates and the giddy pleasure he conveys through the simple visual manipulation of the physical world make him a natural successor to the world's first filmmakers, artists who invented a "cinema of attractions" that was grounded in the wonder and sensuality of the filmgoing experience itself.

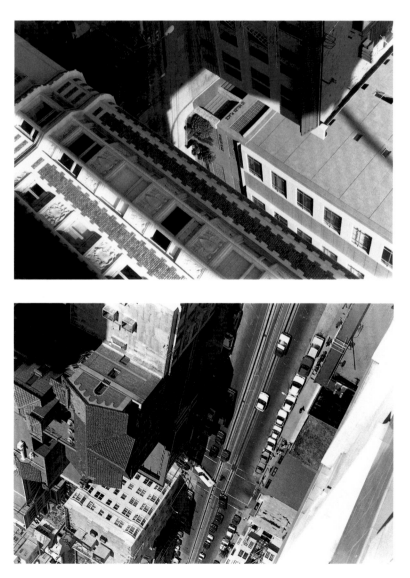

Rea Tajiri.
**History &
Memory**. 1991

Warren Sonbert.
**Short Fuse**. 1991

Clint Eastwood.
**Unforgiven**. 1992.
*Clint Eastwood*

A Western that is at once moody and
ambivalent, comical and cruel, *Unforgiven*
follows its unlikely, unheroic avengers
across a broad, pristine landscape under
bright skies to a frontier town where leg-
end and death by violence are equally
ridiculed. Reformed gunfighter Will
Munny convinces his former partner, Ned
Logan, to join him in killing a man who
slashed a prostitute—a dishonorable task,
but one that will ensure them a substantial
reward and the promise of a peaceful old
age. Bluffing his way in as the third
partner is a rookie outlaw, who survives
the unfolding events and learns a painful
moral truth. The mocking tone of the
dialogue provides a counterpoint to the
Western genre's rhythms of hit, run, and
destroy, and the idea that men who live by
violence can also be brilliantly funny
sharpens director-star Clint Eastwood's
steady gaze. With this film, which instills
a new morality into the traditional
Western, Eastwood single-handedly
revived an entire genre.

Clint Eastwood.
**A Perfect World**.
1993. *Kevin Costner,*
*T. J. Lowther*

Terence Davies.
**The Long Day
Closes.** 1992. *Leigh
McCormack (center)*

Paul McCarthy and
Mike Kelley.
**Heidi.** 1992

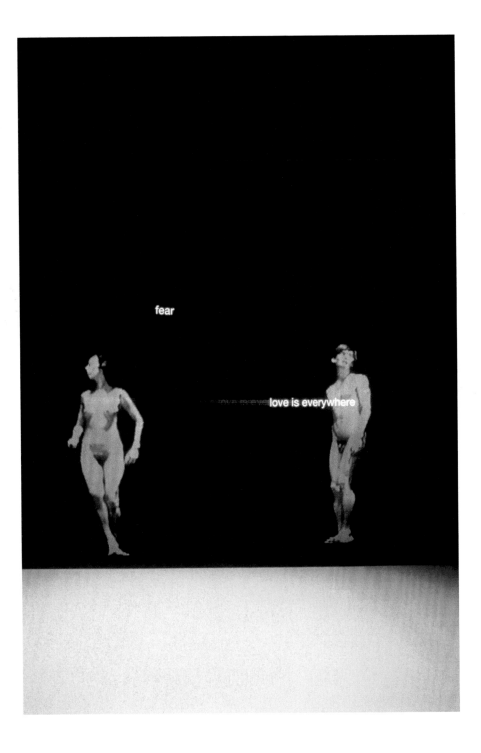

Teiji Furuhashi.
**Lovers**. 1994

*Opposite:*
Martin Scorsese.
**The Age of
Innocence**. 1993.
*Michelle Pfeiffer,
Daniel Day-Lewis*

Quentin Tarantino.
**Pulp Fiction**. 1994.
*Uma Thurman*

After the critical success of 1992's *Reservoir Dogs*—a film so violent that it borders on the pornographic, but filled with knowing references to classic films and film genres that mark it as the work of a knowledgeable and witty cinephile—audiences and critics alike wondered how writer/director Quentin Tarantino could possibly top himself without falling into self-parody. The answer came two years later with *Pulp Fiction*, a film that skillfully shifted attention away from its own considerable violence with unexpected humor, both verbal and visual, and that kept viewers off-kilter with its fragmented narrative structure without in any way thwarting their desire for coherence and resolution. A self-taught student of film history, Tarantino has the uncanny ability to absorb and invoke the work of past filmmakers without plagiarizing them. *Pulp Fiction*, as its very title suggests, portrays a seedy world, but as its title also suggests, it does so with a knowing wink and refusal to take itself too seriously—a ploy that allows Tarantino to load his film with all manner of baroque narrative twists and turns without boring his audience or making them turn away in revulsion. On the contrary, *Pulp Fiction* is the kind of film that audiences find impossible to turn away from, so curious are they to see what could possibly come next. The film spawned many imitators, eager to cash in on what was perceived to be a simple formula, but Tarantino's film is that rare phenomenon: one that tests the boundaries of what is permissible in a mainstream film while actually broadening the audience for formal experimentation.

Ximena Cuevas.
**Corazón sangrante
(Bleeding Heart).**
1993

Cheryl Donegan.
**Head.** 1993

Whit Stillman.
**Barcelona**. 1994.
*Mira Sorvino (far right)*

*Opposite, top:*
Bill Viola.
**Stations**. 1994

*Opposite, bottom:*
Matthew Barney.
**Cremaster 4**. 1994

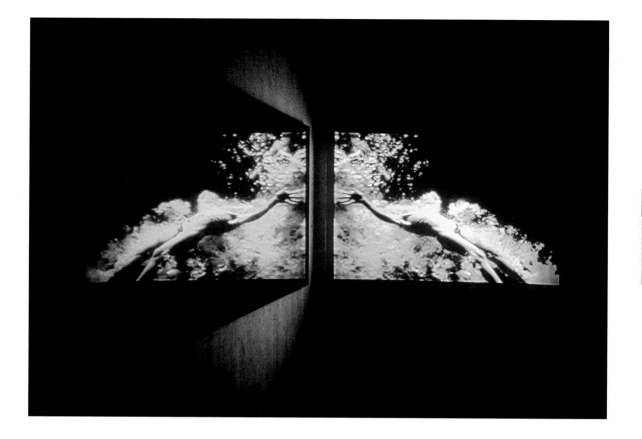

John Lasseter.
**Toy Story**. 1995

When Steve Jobs bought George Lucas's computer-animation division in 1986 and, in partnership with the Walt Disney Company, turned it into Pixar Animation Studios, none but a handful of true believers thought that CGI (computer-generated imagery) technology would be useful for much more than the creation of special effects for the occasional action film. In a few short years, however, the creative team at Pixar—led by Ed Catmull and John Lasseter—proved that CGI could indeed produce animated films of great beauty and imagination, so long as the fundamentals of narrative filmmaking (story, character, and world) were observed and honored. After making a series of influential short films, Lasseter undertook the production of *Toy Story*, the first CGI-only feature ever made. It tells the tale of Buzz Lightyear and Woody, two toys who vie for the affection of Andy, the young boy they belong to. It is a comedy/action film, filled with daring adventures and comic exploits, but at its core *Toy Story* is the tale of two rivals who become friends, as well as a love story about a child and his toys. As Lasseter has so often asserted, Pixar films are not about the technology, but about storytelling. In 2005, in honor of their twentieth anniversary, Pixar and Disney donated the company's entire library of short and feature-length theatrical films to The Museum of Modern Art's permanent collection.

Hal Hartley.
**Amateur**. 1994.
*Elina Löwensohn*

Jem Cohen.
**Lost Book Found**.
1996

John Sayles.
**Lone Star.** 1996.
*Matthew
McConaughey,
Kris Kristofferson*

Joel Coen and
Ethan Coen.
**Fargo**. 1996.
*Frances McDormand*

Whether reimagining Hollywood à la Nathanael West in *Barton Fink* (1991), plumbing the depths of Depression-era noir in *Miller's Crossing* (1990), or adapting Homer for *O Brother, Where Art Thou?* (2000), the Coen brothers duo—Joel directing, Ethan producing, both writing—has consistently managed to draw laughter from material otherwise too sad or hopeless to endure. In all cases, they appropriate genres with abandon so that they may unveil the complexities of the human psyche. In *Fargo* the Coens came up with the perfect combination of form and content, creating a black comedy of unusual scope and resonance. Viewed by some as a scathing attack on the Midwest (but defended by the filmmakers themselves as an homage to the region of their birth), *Fargo* deftly integrates the banal and the bizarre, the tender and the horrific, demonstrating a great affection for its characters while never shying away from the potent stew of seeming contradictions we humans really are.

Ken Jacobs.
**Disorient
Express.** 1995

Dan Boord and
Luis Valdovino.
**Patagonia**. 1996

Stan Brakhage.
**Commingled
Containers.** 1997

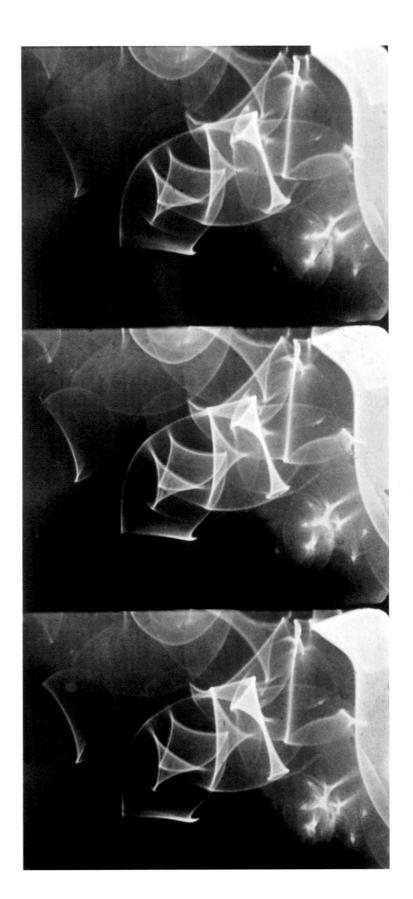

Zhang Peili.
**Eating**. 1997

Lewis Klahr.
**Pony Glass**. 1997

Joan Jonas.
**My New Theater 1**.
1997

Joan Jonas has worked in video and performance for more than thirty years, integrating the two art forms in unexpected ways. *My New Theater 1* continues Jonas's exploration of the dual art form, but on a radically altered scale, resulting in what she has described as "a new effort to create performances in miniature." The setting is a tabletop installation in the form of a box that slopes upward from front to back and is open at one end, allowing the viewer to watch a video screen filling the far wall of the "theater." The video presents a Cape Breton step dancer performing to the accompaniment of a fiddler and a piano player, intercut with a young girl dancing in a more elaborate style. Sparse props—miniature fishing pole, owl, rabbit, chaise longue—litter the maquette. The scale evokes the miniature cities and elongated figures of Alberto Giacometti, whose work has influenced Jonas, and the spirit recalls the New York avant-garde theater companies The Wooster Group—with whom she has frequently collaborated—and Mabou Mines.

Roger Spottiswoode.
**Tomorrow Never
Dies**. 1997. *Pierce
Brosnan, Michelle Yeoh*

Jean-Luc Godard
and Anne-Marie
Miéville.
**The Old Place**.
1999

David Lynch.
**The Straight
Story**. 1999.
*Richard Farnsworth,
Sissy Spacek*

David Lynch's *The Straight Story*, about basic human decency and determination, could be mistaken for a fable were it not a true story. Alvin Straight, a plainspoken seventy-five-year-old man living with his daughter in a small Midwestern American town, learns that his brother, with whom he has not spoken in over a decade, is gravely ill. No longer able to drive a car, he determines to make the three-hundred-mile journey to his brother's home on a riding lawnmower. This story has the potential for satiric swipes at small-town folk as well as pointed jabs at contemporary red-state culture, yet although the film is humorous, it is without irony or cynicism. *The Straight Story* is, for Lynch, a most eccentric film—unlike virtually every other film he has made, it refuses to engage in narrative legerdemain or visual tomfoolery. It assumes its characters' points of view, and in so doing presents itself straight and unadorned. There is never really any doubt that despite the several setbacks he encounters, Alvin will eventually arrive at his brother's front door. When he does, the result is as uneventful and deeply affecting as everyday life.

David Williams.
**Thirteen**. 1997.
*Nina Dickens*

Pipilotti Rist.
**Ever Is Over All**.
1997

Jia Zhang Ke.
**Xiao Wu**. 1997.
*Zhao Tao*

Xiao Wu is a pickpocket in Fenyang, a small provincial town in China. He is one of life's many losers, a man who cannot seem to connect with those around him and who is apparently oblivious to the changes, both economic and social, that are the hallmark of contemporary China. He takes up with Mei Mei, a young prostitute, but she soon drops him, and he is cast adrift, a victim of his own inability to cope with anything outside his immediate environment. Having been under pressure from the police to curb his thievery, he is finally arrested and taken away. There is no catharsis in the film's final frames, nor is there any sense that Xiao Wu is truly aware of how he has ended up the way he has. His interior reality and the outside world do not intersect, and so our "hero" is left to ponder his fate helplessly. First-time director Jia Zhang Ke made *Xiao Wu* on a minuscule budget, filming in the familiar confines of his hometown and using a cast of nonprofessionals. He also failed to get official permission to make the film, giving the movie the distinction of being an independent, underground film in a country where such activity can carry a heavy penalty, both personal and professional. *Xiao Wu*'s international success protected Jia somewhat, but can in no way minimize the fact that he and his entire company risked a great deal to create it.

Whit Stillman.
**The Last Days of
Disco**. 1998.
*Kate Beckinsale,
Chloë Sevigny*

Alexander Payne.
**Election**. 1999.
*Reese Witherspoon*

Al Pacino.
**Looking for
Richard**. 1996.
*Al Pacino,
Kevin Spacey*

David O. Russell.
**Three Kings**.
1999. *George
Clooney, Ice Cube,
Mark Wahlberg*

Seoungho Cho.
**Cold Pieces**. 1999

Korean-born Seoungho Cho creates video works that are almost painterly in their presentation of intricately textured surfaces, yet at the same time uniquely time-based in their reliance on the play of light across those surfaces. In *Cold Pieces* he trains his camera on water, a substance without an identifiable shape or size. Water pours from a faucet, drops of rain splash in a puddle, waves roll across the frame. In its many and diverse variations, water as represented in this eleven-minute work becomes a metaphor for motion itself. Sound and image are joined together in a subtle collage that explores the very concept of movement from source to destination. Simple in means, *Cold Pieces* is nevertheless a work of complex lyricism, one that challenges the viewer to derive deep meaning from seemingly mundane images.

Tom Kalin.
**Third Known
Nest.** 1999

# 2000s

Terence Davies.
**The House of
Mirth**. 2000.
*Gillian Anderson*

*Opposite:*
Laurence Attali.
**Baobab**. 2000

Orlando Mesquita.
**The Ball**. 2001

An AIDS public service announcement produced by the international advocacy group Steps for the Future, Orlando Mesquita's short film *The Ball* presents a surprisingly lighthearted view of condom use in Africa. In a village in Mozambique, a man interrupts a group of boys playing soccer and accuses them of stealing his condoms to make soccer balls. Determined to carry on playing, the boys go off to buy a new condom for another ball. The ball is ingeniously constructed by wrapping the inflated condom first in a plastic bag and then in a piece of cloth, and tying it up with string. When they run out of string, the boys make use of a baby's jacket hanging out to dry on a clothesline, unraveling the wool from a loose strand. Mesquita has made more than thirty films over a twenty-year career, including fiction features, documentaries, and educational programs, yet none have had quite as popular an impact as this whimsical piece of social advocacy.

Kristin Lucas.
**Five Minute
Break.** 2001

Faith Hubley.
**Witch Madness.**
2000

Wu Wenguang.
**Dance with Farm Workers**. 2002

Bill Morrison.
**Decasia**. 2001

*Opposite:*
Sofia Coppola.
**Lost in Translation**.
2003. *Bill Murray, Scarlett Johansson*

Nathaniel Kahn.
**My Architect**.
2003

When architect Louis I. Kahn died suddenly in New York's Pennsylvania Station in 1974, he was seventy-three years old and deeply in debt, and he left behind three families—one legitimate, the other two not. Nathaniel, born of one of Kahn's mistresses, was the youngest survivor, only eleven years old when his father died. *My Architect* is the adult Nathaniel's attempt finally to come to terms with his father's life and work. The film approaches the elder Kahn in two ways, through his buildings and through interviews with those who knew him best: family, colleagues, and acquaintances. Nathaniel visits and films himself interacting with such famous structures as the Salk Institute for Biological Studies in La Jolla, California, the capitol building in Dhaka, Bangladesh,

and the library at the Phillips Exeter Academy in Exeter, New Hampshire. Architecture luminaries I. M. Pei, Philip Johnson, Robert A. M. Stern, and Frank Gehry, among others, speak to Nathaniel about his father's professional methods and legacy, as well as about his troubled personal life. The most affecting footage is of Nathaniel's mother and his two siblings, testimony that is all too brief and on which he fails to elaborate, but which nevertheless provides much-needed insight into the personality of the famous man. In the end, Nathaniel Kahn never does gain full knowledge and understanding of his father, yet he does achieve a kind of grudging peace within himself, as well as a deeper appreciation of his father's considerable achievements.

# The Celeste Bartos Film Preservation Center

After fifty years of actively building its collection, The Museum of Modern Art realized in the mid-1980s that the size of its permanent film collection and the collection's special conservation needs would preclude their being stored at the Museum in midtown Manhattan. Mary Lea Bandy, then the recently appointed director of the Department of Film, approached Celeste Bartos, chair of the Trustee Committee on Film, with the idea of creating an off-site facility to house the collection.

Ten years later, on June 20, 1996, the Museum opened the Celeste Bartos Film Preservation Center, a state-of-the-art facility in Hamlin, Pennsylvania. The Center comprises two buildings on a wooded thirty-eight-acre

View of main building, 1996

*The Goddess of Sagebrush Gulch*

**Conference Room**

*Above:*
An example of signage created
for the Bartos Center rooms.
Each room bears the name of a
Biograph Company film in the
Museum's collections.

*Above, left:*
View of workroom,
1996

*Above:*
View of typical
safety-film vault,
1996

*Left:*
View of special-
collections vault,
1996

estate: a 7,900-square-foot facility for the
Museum's fragile nitrate films, which date from
1894 to 1951, and a much larger, 28,000-
square-foot main building, which houses the
acetate-based films.

Film is a fragile medium. If improperly
stored, it will shrink, crack, turn gummy, or
congeal into an inseparable mass. The color and
imagery fades, the magnetic sound track flakes
off the film base, and the film itself breaks apart.
Eventually, the film disintegrates and turns to
dust. Only cool, stable storage conditions
discourage fading and deterioration. For these

reasons, the Center offers a flexible system of
temperature- and humidity-controlled vaults
with the ability to adapt as the collection
increases and preservation techniques advance.

Each of the Center's fifty-eight vaults has its
own climate controls, since different types of
film (black-and-white prints and negatives,
color prints and negatives, fine-grain masters)
have different needs. Temperatures vary from
thirty-five to fifty-five degrees Fahrenheit, and
humidity levels are kept uniformly low. The
nearly one hundred thousand cans of film in the
Museum's collections are stored according to

View of nitrate
building, 1996

size, type, and format, which ranges from 8mm to 70mm. The main building, which houses safety films, contains eighteen vaults on two floors, and the nitrate building contains thirty-four vaults, each capable of holding approximately one million feet of film. The main building also houses three vaults for the nonfilm components of the collection, such as posters, production notes, books, periodicals, and photographs, as well as the video collection.

The John D. and Catherine T. MacArthur Foundation provided a planning grant for the Center, and major funding was provided by Celeste Bartos, Sony Corporation of America, the National Endowment for the Arts, Dorothy and Lewis B. Cullman, the Hartley Ramsay Estate, the Lillian Gish Trust, Time Warner Inc., David Rockefeller, Agnes Gund, George Gund III, Mercedes and Sid R. Bass, Jerry I. Speyer, Caral and M. Joseph Lebworth, and Twentieth Century Fox. All members of the Museum's Board of Trustees contributed to the project.

View of nitrate
building corridor,
1996

View of typical
nitrate-film vault,
1996

*The Tragedy of a Dress Suit*

N20

A sign for one of the
nitrate vaults

# Index of Films

This list contains the films and videos included in this book. It was compiled by Steven Higgins, Curator in the Department of Film and Media, and Brynn White, Intern. Additional help was provided by Barbara London, Associate Curator; Sally Berger, Assistant Curator; Peter Williamson, Film Conservation Manager; and Maholo Uchida, Intern.

It is arranged alphabetically by filmmaker/artist and then chronologically by year of release. In the case of foreign-language works, the original release title is given first, followed by the English-language release title (if any). All filmographic and videographic data are drawn from, and have been checked against, the Museum's own cataloging records. For an explanation of the difference between preservation and restoration, see pages 9–11.

**Harry d'Abbadie d'Arrast**
*Laughter.* 1930 [page 150]
USA. 35mm print, black and white, sound, 79 min. Acquired from the Museum of the City of New York

**Rhonda Abrams**
*The Lament of the Sugar Bush Man.* 1987 [page 304]
Canada. 1" video, color, sound, 15 min. Acquired from the artist

**Vito Acconci**
*Theme Song.* 1973 [page 260]
USA. ¾" video, black and white, sound, 79 min. Gift of the artist

**Peggy Ahwesh**
*Martina's Playhouse.* 1989 [page 311]
USA. Super-8mm print, color, sound, 20 min. Acquired from the artist

**Woody Allen**
*Zelig.* 1983 [page 294]
USA. 35mm print, black and white and color, sound, 79 min. Acquired from the artist
*Broadway Danny Rose.* 1984 [page 290]
USA. 35mm print, black and white, sound, 84 min. Acquired from the artist

**Laurie Anderson**
*O Superman.* 1983 [page 288]
USA. ½" video, color, sound, 8 min. Gift of Warner Bros. Records

**Ant Farm**
*Media Burn.* 1975 [page 268]
USA. ¾" video, color, sound, 26 min. Gift of Celeste Bartos

**Eleanor Antin**
*From the Archives of Modern Art.* 1987 [page 304]
USA. ¾" video, black and white, sound, 24 min. Gift of the Richard Florsheim Art Fund

**Michelangelo Antonioni**
*Il deserto rosso (Red Desert).* 1964 [page 239]
Italy/France. 35mm print, color, sound, 117 min. Acquired from Mediaset S.p.A.

**Roscoe Arbuckle**
*Fatty and Mabel Adrift.* 1916 [page 54]
USA. 35mm print, black and white, silent, approx. 30 min.

**Ray Ashley, Morris Engel, and Ruth Orkin**
*Little Fugitive.* 1953 [page 219]
USA. 35mm print, black and white, sound, 75 min. Indefinite loan from Morris Engel. Restored with funding from The Film Foundation/Hollywood Foreign Press Association

**Anthony Asquith**
*Underground.* 1928 [page 134]
Great Britain. 35mm print, black and white, silent, approx. 77 min. Acquired from the National Film and Television Archive/British Film Institute

**Charles Atlas and Merce Cunningham**
*Blue Studio.* 1976 [page 269]
USA. ¾" video, color, sound, 15 min. Gift of Barbara Pine

**Laurence Attali**
*Baobab.* 2000 [page 351]
Senegal. 35mm print, color, sound, 25 min. Acquired from the artist

**Beth B.**
*The Dominatrix Sleeps Tonight.* 1984 [page 291]
USA. ¾" video, color, sound, 4 min. Gift of Barbara Pine

**Hector Babenco**
*Pixote.* 1980 [page 278]
Brazil. 35 mm print, color, sound, 127 min. Indefinite loan from Dan Talbot/New Yorker Films

**Clarence G. Badger**
*Jubilo.* 1919 [page 73]
USA. 35mm print, black and white, silent, approx. 61 min. Acquired from Metro-Goldwyn-Mayer
*It.* 1927 [page 122]
USA. 16mm print, black and white, silent, approx. 72 min. Acquired from Charles L. Turner

**John Baldessari**
*I Am Making Art.* 1971 [page 253]
USA. ¾" video, black and white, sound, 19 min. Gift of Barbara Pine

**Reginald Barker**
*The Coward.* 1915 [page 53]
USA. 35mm print, black and white, silent, 70 min. Preserved with funding from the National Endowment for the Arts and National Film Preservation Foundation

**Matthew Barney**
*Cremaster 4.* 1994 [page 331]
USA/France/Great Britain. Laser disc in presentation box (plastic, satin, fabric), color, sound, 42 min. Acquired with funding from the Blanchette Hooker Rockefeller Fund Bequest

**Herbert J. Biberman**
*Salt of the Earth.* 1954 [page 221]
USA. 35mm print, black and white, silent, approx. 90 min. Gift of Paul Jarrico

**Kathryn Bigelow**
*Near Dark.* 1987 [page 301]
USA. 35mm print, color, sound, 94 min. Gift of the artist

**G. W. Bitzer**
*Westinghouse Works.* 1904 [page 30]
USA. 35mm print, black and white, silent, approx. 17 min. Gift of Actinograph Corp.
*Interior N.Y. Subway, 14th Street to 42nd Street.* 1905 [page 29]
USA. 35mm print, black and white, silent, approx. 4 min. Gift of Actinograph Corp.

**Dan Boord and Luis Valdovino**
*Patagonia.* 1996 [page 338]
USA/Argentina. ¾" video, color, sound, 29 min. Gift of the artists

**Lizzie Borden**
*Born in Flames.* 1983 [page 291]
USA. 16mm print, color, sound, 90 min. Acquired from the artist.

**Frank Borzage**
*Humoresque.* 1920 [page 78]
USA. 35mm print, black and

**Clint Eastwood**
*Unforgiven.* 1992 [page 323]
    USA. 35mm print, color, sound,
    130 min. Gift of the artist and
    Warner Bros.
*A Perfect World.* 1993 [page 324]
    USA. 35mm print, color, sound,
    137 min. Gift of the artist and
    Warner Bros.

**Sergei Eisenstein**
*Bronenosets Potemkin (Potemkin; Battleship Potemkin).* 1925 [page 106]
    Soviet Union. 35mm print, black
    and white and hand colored,
    silent, approx. 75 min. Acquired
    from Reichsfilmarchiv
*Oktyabr' (October; Ten Days That Shook the World).* 1928 [page 135]
    Soviet Union. 35mm print, black
    and white, silent, approx. 103 min.
    Acquired from Gosfilmofond
*¡Que viva Mexico!* 1931 [page 156]
    USA/Mexico. 35mm print, black
    and white, silent, unedited
    footage. Gift of Upton Sinclair
*Alexander Nevsky.* 1938 [page 171]
    Soviet Union. 35mm print, black
    and white, sound, 108 min. Indefinite loan from Janus Films
*Ivan Grozny (Ivan the Terrible).* 1945
    [page 201]
    Soviet Union. 35mm print, black
    and white, sound, 205 min. in two
    parts, 120 min. and 85 min.
    Acquired from Gosfilmofond

**John Emerson**
*Wild & Woolly.* 1917 [page 90]
    USA. 35mm print, black and
    white, silent, approx. 73 min. Gift
    of Douglas Fairbanks. Restored
    with funding from the National
    Film Preservation Foundation
    and The Film Foundation

**Ed Emshwiller**
*Scape-Mates.* 1972 [page 256]
    USA. 16mm print, color, sound,
    29 min. Gift of the American
    Film Institute

**Jean Epstein**
*Coeur fidèle.* 1923 [page 88]
    France. 35mm print, black and
    white, silent, approx. 80 min. Preserved from original materials on
    loan from Cinémathèque Royale,
    Brussels
*La Chute de la maison Usher (The Fall of the House of Usher).* 1928
    [page 130]
    France. 35mm print, black and
    white, silent, approx. 63 min. Preserved from original materials on
    loan from Cinémathèque
    Française

**Rainer Werner Fassbinder**
*Die Ehe der Maria Braun (The Marriage of Maria Braun).* 1978
    [page 275]
    West Germany. 35mm print, black
    and white, sound, 104 min.
    Acquired from the Rainer Werner
    Fassbinder Foundation
*Die Sehnsucht der Veronika Voss (Veronica Voss).* 1982 [page 286]
    West Germany. 35mm print, black
    and white, sound, 104 min.
    Acquired from the Rainer Werner
    Fassbinder Foundation

**Federico Fellini**
*Lo sceicco bianco (The White Sheik).*
    1952 [page 215]
    Italy. 35mm print, black and
    white, sound, 91 min. Acquired
    from Mediaset S.p.A.
*I vitelloni.* 1953 [page 220]
    Italy. 35mm print, black and
    white, sound, 105 min. Acquired
    from Mediaset S.p.A.
*La dolce vita.* 1960 [page 234]
    France/Italy. 35mm print, black
    and white, sound, 175 min.
    Acquired from Mediaset S.p.A.
*8½.* 1963 [page 238]
    Italy. 35mm print, black and
    white, sound, 135 min. Acquired
    from Mediaset S.p.A.
*Giulietta degli spiriti (Juliet of the Spirits).* 1965 [page 241]
    Italy. 35mm print, color, sound,
    137 min. Acquired from Mediaset
    S.p.A.

**Oskar Fischinger**
*Motion Painting I.* 1947 [page 204]
    USA. 35mm print, color, silent,
    approx. 11 min. Gift of Walt Disney Pictures. Restored with funding from the Celeste Bartos Film
    Preservation Fund

**Robert J. Flaherty**
*Nanook of the North.* 1922 [page 82]
    USA. 35mm print, black and white
    and color tinted, silent, approx. 56
    min. Acquired from the artist.
    Restored with funding from the
    Celeste Bartos Film Preservation
    Fund and the National Endowment for the Arts
*Moana.* 1926 [page 114]
    USA. 35mm print, black and
    white, silent, approx. 35 min.
    Acquired from the artist. Restored
    with funding from the National
    Film Preservation Foundation and
    The Film Foundation/Hollywood
    Foreign Press Association
*Man of Aran.* 1934 [page 164]
    Great Britain. 35mm print, black
    and white, sound, 75 min.
*The Land.* 1942 [page 192]
    USA. 35mm print, black and

white, sound, 42 min. Acquired
from the artist. Restored with
funding from the Celeste Bartos
Film Preservation Fund and The
Film Foundation
*Louisiana Story.* 1948 [page 210]
    USA. 35mm print, black and
    white, sound, 79 min. Gift of the
    artist

**Dave Fleischer**
*Inklings, Issue 12.* 1927 [page 119]
    USA. 35mm print, black and
    white, silent, approx. 6 min. Gift
    of the American Film Institute

**Victor Fleming**
*The Mollycoddle.* 1920 [page 91]
    USA. 35mm print, black and
    white, silent, approx. 81 min. Gift
    of Douglas Fairbanks. Restored
    with funding from the National
    Film Preservation Foundation and
    The Film Foundation
*When the Clouds Roll By.* 1919
    [page 92]
    USA. 35mm print, black and
    white, silent, approx. 86 min. Gift
    of Douglas Fairbanks. Preserved
    with funding from the Richard
    Griffith Memorial Fund

**Victor Fleming and
Douglas Fairbanks**
*Around the World in Eighty Minutes with Douglas Fairbanks.* 1931
    [page 98]
    USA. 35mm print, black and
    white, sound, 78 min. Gift of
    Douglas Fairbanks

**Robert Florey**
*The Life and Death of 9413—A Hollywood Extra.* 1928 [page 124]
    USA. 35mm print, black and
    white, silent, approx. 11 min.
    Acquired from Cinema Arts. Preserved with funding from the
    Celeste Bartos Film Preservation
    Fund

**Peter Fonda**
*The Hired Hand.* 1971 [page 252]
    USA. 35mm print, color, sound,
    90 min. Acquired from Frank
    Mazzola

**John Ford**
*Straight Shooting.* 1917 [page 70]
    USA. 35mm print, black and
    white, silent, approx. 57 min. Gift
    of Jugoslovenska Kinoteka, Belgrade
*The Iron Horse.* 1924 [page 100]
    USA. 16mm print, black and
    white, silent, approx. 114 min.
    Gift of Twentieth Century–Fox.
    Preserved with funding from the
    Celeste Bartos Film Preservation
    Fund and The Film Foundation

*Hangman's House.* 1928 [page 127]
    USA. 35mm print, black and
    white, silent, approx. 71 min. Gift
    of Twentieth Century–Fox. Preserved with funding from the
    National Endowment for the Arts
*Up the River.* 1930 [page 148]
    USA. 35mm print, black and
    white, sound, 85 min. Gift of
    Twentieth Century–Fox
*Stagecoach.* 1939 [page 179]
    USA. 35mm print, black and
    white, sound, 93 min. Gift of
    AFP Exchange
*How Green Was My Valley.* 1941
    [page 182]
    USA. 16mm print, black and
    white, sound, 118 min. Acquired
    from Twentieth Century–Fox
*My Darling Clementine.* 1946
    [page 203]
    USA. 35mm print, color, sound,
    97 min. Gift of Twentieth
    Century–Fox. Preserved with
    funding from the National
    Endowment for the Humanities
*The Searchers.* 1956 [page 228]
    USA. 35mm print, color, sound,
    119 min. Gift of Warner Bros.

**Hermine Freed**
*Art Herstory.* 1974 [page 264]
    USA. ½" video, color, sound, 22
    min. Acquired from the artist and
    Video Data Bank

**Masaki Fujihata**
*Maitreya.* 1984 [page 295]
    Japan. ¼" video, color, sound, 4
    min. Gift of the artist

**Teiji Furuhashi**
*Lovers.* 1994 [page 326]
    USA. Video installation with five
    laser discs and players, five projectors, two sound systems, two slide
    projectors, and two computers,
    11'6" x 32'10" x 32'10" (350.5 x
    1,000.8 x 1,000.8 cm). Gift of
    Canon Inc.

**Henrik Galeen**
*Der Student von Prag (The Student of Prague).* 1926 [page 113]
    Germany. 35mm print, black and
    white, silent, approx. 58 min.
    Acquired from the Filmmuseum
    im Münchner Stadtmuseum

**Abel Gance**
*La Roue.* 1923 [page 88]
    France. 35mm print, black and
    white, silent, approx. 195 min.
    Acquired from Cinémathèque
    Française and Images Film
    Archive

**Index of Films**

**William A. Wellman**
*Wings.* 1927 [page 121]
　　USA. 35mm print, black and
　　white, silent, approx. 141 min.
　　Gift of Paramount Pictures
*Nothing Sacred.* 1937 [page 186]
　　USA. 35mm print, color, sound,
　　74 minutes. Gift of Selznick Inter-
　　national Pictures. Preserved with
　　funding from the Celeste Bartos
　　Film Preservation Fund

**Leopold Wharton**
*Patria.* 1917 [page 71]
　　USA. 35mm print, black and
　　white, silent, approx. 60 min.
　　(excerpt). Acquired from C. B.
　　Stratton/Cosmopolitan
　　Productions

**James White and William Heise**
*Fatima's Coochee-Coochee Dance.* 1896
　　[page 17]
　　USA. 35mm print, black and
　　white, silent, approx. 90 sec.
*Sun Dance—Annabelle.* 1897
　　[page 15]
　　USA. 35mm print, black and
　　white, silent, approx. 30 sec.

**Ted Wilde**
*Speedy.* 1928 [page 138]
　　USA. 35mm print, black and
　　white, silent, approx. 62 min.
　　Acquired from Ceskoslovensky
　　Filmovy Archiv

**C. Jay Williams**
*The Totville Eye.* 1912 [page 21]
　　USA. 35mm print, black and
　　white, silent, approx. 13 min. Gift
　　of R. L. Giffen. Preserved with
　　funding from the National
　　Endowment for the Arts

**David Williams**
*Thirteen.* 1997 [page 344]
　　USA. 16mm print, color, sound,
　　87 min. Acquired from the artist

**James Williamson**
*The Big Swallow.* 1901 [page 24]
　　Great Britain. 35mm print, black
　　and white, silent, approx. 35 sec.
　　Acquired from the National Film
　　and Television Archive/British
　　Film Institute

**Robert Wilson**
*Deafman Glance.* 1981 [page 280]
　　USA. ¼" video, color, sound, 27
　　min. Acquired from the artist and
　　the Byrd Hoffman Foundation Inc.

**John Griffith Wray**
*Anna Christie.* 1923 [page 86]
　　USA. 35mm print, black and
　　white, silent, approx. 96 min.

Acquired from Jugoslovenska
Kinoteka, Belgrade

**Wu Wenguang**
*Dance with Farm Workers.* 2002
　　[page 354]
　　China. 1" video, color, sound, 57
　　min. Acquired from the artist

**William Wyler**
*The Best Years of Our Lives.* 1946
　　[page 201]
　　USA. 16mm print, black and white,
　　sound, 174 min. Acquired from
　　Samuel Goldwyn Productions

**Julie Zando**
*Let's Play Prisoners.* 1988 [page 304]
　　USA. ¼" video, black and white,
　　sound, 22 min. Acquired from the
　　artist

**Zhang Peili**
*Eating.* 1997 [page 340]
　　China. Video installation with
　　three laser discs, three players, and
　　three matching stacked monitors,
　　sound, dimensions variable. Gift
　　of The Junior Associates of the
　　Museum of Modern Art

# Photograph Credits

All of the images used in this book come from the Film Stills Archive of The Museum of Modern Art, with the exception of the following:

Anthology Film Archives: 222; 223; 224 all; 225 all.

Kino International: 14; 17 right; 19 top; 20 all; 21 all.

The National Film Preservation Foundation: 29; 30 all; 55 top; 110.

Information regarding rights holders, where known, is included below. Persons with additional information about rights holders are encouraged to contact the Museum.

Rhonda Abrams: 304 top right.

Vito Acconci: 260 top.

Peggy Ahwesh: 311.

Woody Allen: 290; 294 top.

American Zoetrope: 355.

Laurie Anderson: 288.

Eleanor Antin: 304 bottom.

Laurence Attali: 351.

Beth B.: 291 bottom.

John Baldessari: 253 bottom.

Matthew Barney: 331 bottom.

Kathryn Bigelow: 301.

Dan Boord and Luis Valdovino: 338.

Lizzie Borden: 291 top.

Marilyn Brakhage: 263; 339.

British Film Institute and Channel Four Films: 325 top.

David Byrne and Stephen Johnson: 295 bottom.

Peter Callas: 310 bottom.

Peter Campus: 261; 270 bottom.

Castle Rock Entertainment: 330; 346 top.

Abigail Child: 300 top.

Seoungho Cho: 348 bottom.

Wendy Clarke: 281 bottom.

Jem Cohen: 333 bottom.

Cecilia Condit: 283 top.

Ximena Cuevas: 329 top.

Merce Cunningham: 269.

Dominant 7 Productions: 352.

Cheryl Donegan: 329 bottom.

Nathaniel Dorsky: 302 top.

Carol Emshwiller: 256.

Mary Engel: 219.

Rainer Werner Fassbinder Foundation: 275 top; 286 top.

Elfriede Fischinger Trust: 204.

Hermine Freed: 264 bottom.

Masaki Fujihata: 295 top.

Teiji Furuhashi: 326.

Ernie Gehr: 250; 321.

Gilbert and George: 257 bottom.

Shalom Gorewitz: 292.

Dan Graham: 289.

Hal Hartley: 333 top.

Mona Hatoum: 307 bottom.

James Herbert: 251 bottom.

Gary Hill: 307 top; 310 top; 316.

Emily Hubley: 353 bottom.

Joy Hurwitz: 253 top.

Mako Idemitsu: 291 middle.

Ken Jacobs: 336–37.

Janus Films/The Criterion Collection: 153; 170 top left; 170 bottom; 174; 195; 201 bottom right; 202 top; 205 bottom; 214 top; 232; 235 bottom; 241 bottom; 259; 293.

Jerome Foundation; 231 bottom; 255.

Joan Jonas: 258 top; 294 bottom; 341.

Nathaniel Kahn: 356.

Tom Kalin: 349.

Kino International: 318.

Lewis Klahr: 340 bottom.

Paul Kos: 254 top.

George Kuchar: 300 bottom.

Kristin Lucas: 353 top.

Mary Lucier: 302 bottom.

Chris Marker: 320.

Victor Masayesva: 296 top.

Paul McCarthy and Mike Kelley: 325 bottom.

Mediaset S.p.A.: 214 bottom; 215; 220; 234; 238; 239 bottom; 241 top.

Merchant Ivory Productions: 229; 236.

Metro-Goldwyn-Mayer: 227 top; 248; 285; 299; 342 top.

Milestone Film and Video: 120 top.

Miramax: 328.

MK2 Productions: 357.

Linda Montano: 272 bottom.

Bill Morrison: 354 bottom.

Antonio Muntadas: 317 top.

The Museum of Modern Art: 222; 224 left; 225 all; 342 bottom.

National Film Board of Canada: 211.

Bruce Nauman: 249 bottom.

National Broadcasting Company (NBC): 217 bottom right.

New Yorker Films: 298 bottom.

Marcel Odenbach: 287.

Tony Oursler: 278 top.

Nam June Paik Studios: 258 bottom; 268 bottom.

Paper Tiger Television: 281 top.

Paramount Pictures: 121; 129 bottom; 231 top; 267 top; 277; 346 bottom.

P.P. Film Polski: 282.

Radiotelevisione Italiana (RAI): 286 bottom.

Susan Raymond and Alan Raymond: 272 top.

Pipilotti Rist: 344 bottom.

RKO Pictures: 317 bottom.

Martha Rosler: 266.

Chiz Schultz: 260 bottom.

Martin Scorsese: 265.

Richard Serra: 262 top.

Bill Sherwood: 298 top.

Shochiku Films Ltd.: 218 top.

Shelly Silver: 319.

Société des Etablissements L. Gaumont: 306.

Warren Sonbert: 322 bottom.

Keith Sonnier: 257 top.

Sony Pictures Entertainment: 158 bottom; 163 bottom; 178 top; 213 bottom; 217 top; 221 top; 226; 240; 271; 327; 334; 350.

Lisa Steele: 264 top.

Strand Releasing Corp.: 237 top.

John Sturgeon: 274 top.

Rea Tajiri: 322 top.

Leslie Thornton: 296 bottom.

Twentieth Century Fox: 120 bottom; 125; 126 bottom; 127; 131; 144; 148 top; 160 bottom; 182 top; 183; 197 bottom; 203; 207 bottom; 213 top; 347.

United Artists: 161 bottom; 163 top; 168 bottom; 176 top; 276.

Universal Pictures: 140 bottom; 142; 146; 150 left; 159; 162; 175; 181 bottom; 205 top; 252; 267 bottom; 309; 312; 313.

Johanna VanDerBeek: 237 top.

Melvin Van Peebles: 254 bottom.

Dan Van Vliet: 251 top.

Steina Vasulka: 274 bottom.

Woody Vasulka: 303.

Edin Vélez: 283 bottom.

Bill Viola: 270 top; 273; 284; 331 top.

Walt Disney Pictures: 158 top; 177 top right; 186; 187 bottom; 188; 190; 191; 343.

Walt Disney Pictures and Pixar Animation Studios: 332.

The Andy Warhol Museum: 242; 243; 244; 245; 246 bottom; 247.

Warner Bros. Pictures: 123; 129 top left; 132 bottom; 140 top; 166; 172; 173 top; 176 bottom; 177 bottom; 182 bottom; 185; 189; 192; 193; 197 top; 200 bottom; 201 bottom left; 206 bottom; 207 top; 208; 216; 218 bottom; 228; 237 bottom; 314; 323; 324; 348 top.

William Wegman: 262 bottom.

David Williams: 344 top.

Robert Wilson: 280.

Working Title Films: 335.

Wu Wenguang: 354 top.

Julie Zando: 304 top left.

Zeitgeist Films: 315.

Zhang Peili: 340 top.